Babel Erased:

The Story of Language & History

Babel Erased:

The Story of Language & History

Harry Conway

The Pentland Press Limited
Edinburgh · Cambridge · Durham

© Harry Conway 1994

First published in 1994 by
The Pentland Press Ltd.
1 Hutton Close
South Church
Bishop Auckland
Durham

All rights reserved.
Unauthorised duplication
contravenes existing laws.

ISBN 1 85821 085 2

Typeset by Elite Typesetting Techniques, Southampton.
Printed and bound by Antony Rowe Ltd., Chippenham.

This work is dedicated to the memory of
Dr Lazarus Ludwig Zamenhof
(1859–1917)

The Jewish Inventor of Esperanto

It would not have been possible without the splendid assistance of my daughter Mrs Anita Bernstein, BA (Hons.), my dear friend, Mrs Sally Lyndon, and my niece, Mrs Dot Swarc, BA (Hons.). I owe a deep sense of gratitude to R. G. Collingwood and Giambattista Vico, the great historians.

I am aware that there are many errors of omission which are, of course, my responsibility, largely due, I fear, to my immobility due to my amputated right leg, which confines me to a wheelchair. I hope, however that the errors are not too numerous and that the general reader will find this work of interest.

HARRY CONWAY
MA, AIL, BA
University Diploma:
1. Economics
2. History (Hons.)

Publisher's Note

Sadly, Harry Conway
did not live to see the publication
of *Babel Erased* and it is
with great respect that we dedicate
this book to his memory.

Chapter 1

The general process of history in our society is that process which is a result of the actions and reactions, towards each other, of the various professional, working and ethnic groups, of which the society is composed.

These actions and reactions are motivated by thought, which is expressed in language. Thus thought is the cement which binds together action and language. The causality of language and history is established.

Ethnicity is a comparatively new development in our society but maintaining equilibrium between convergence and divergence is of vital importance. Convergence of ethnicity leads to peace and harmony as in the case of Czechs and Slovaks, who have formed their own states but live in peace and friendship. In Yugoslavia, however, the divergence of ethnicity between Serbs, Croats and Muslims has led to ethnic cleansing, i.e., mass genocide.

Causality of Language and History: What is History?

History is a story, it is a story about the lives of people, men, women and children, in different types of societies, in different stages of development.

Historians are divided into two groups – one group maintains that the function of the historian is that of a chronicler or narrator; he or she records the facts of the period under examination and very often provides brilliant and enthralling literature as a result. Outstanding examples of it are historians like Macaulay and Bryant who really show that certainly the story is an important component of history; whether it is the only one is something we shall have to consider.

But is history only *his* story? Is it the story of the activities, achievements and efforts of men exclusively, wherein the contributions of women are discounted and even denigrated? In any case, of hardly any real value.

How does the language itself reflect the opposing views of the sexes? Feminists maintain that language shows heavily accented male domination and discrimination. They cite a number of instances and in support of their view let us take the words *governor* and *governess*: *governor* indicates a male exercising great power and possessing a dominant personality, and he could show this in various economic, political and scientific fields. His very appearance in many cases would command deference and respect. What however is the general reaction to the word *governess*? A woman in charge of small children – hardly a position of power. Even women would smile at this idea, as they have become accustomed over the centuries to accept their lot as inevitable and unchangeable.

Let us consider another important word – *director*: a male executive, enjoying a position of authority; there is not a word *directoress*. When, as sometimes happens, women with great ability appear, this ability is recognised by their promotion to the position of director; they have acquired masculine attributes in spite of their femininity. Men can think of nothing greater: 'Higher praise than this hath no man.' We note *man* not *person*.

Returning now to our consideration of historians as narrators, we find there is a very serious drawback to overcome and this is the enormous number of facts which are available. One German professor of history spent the whole of his life examining the history of Germany during the four years of 1525–1529. The narrator has to make a selection, and he will do this according to his estimation of their importance. Other historians will apply the same method in making their selection. This explains why historians dealing with the same period will arrive at diametrically opposite conclusions.

We find therefore that the concept of historians as narrators is flawed – history is a story but there are other important factors and in order to appreciate them we require to have a philosophy.

Does this mean that there is a general historical process? It is difficult to see how we can evaluate movements in society if there is not. Macaulay and Bryant can write brilliant and enthralling literature, but this does not get us to the heart of things. For this we must look to the historical philosophers such as Marx, Hegel and Collingwood.

Marx's theory of dialectical materialism is monistic – it is matter that matters! Contradiction is the law of life – ethical considerations do not apply. In society the class war between capital and labour continues but must end in the victory of labour: 'The stars in their courses foretell it.'

Marx boasted that he had stood Hegel on his head. Hegel's philosophical theory is also monistic but based on ethical consideration and he arrived at the conclusion that the Prussian State embodied the highest principles of social justice. It is possible that Hegel was particularly motivated by his desire to obtain a professorship at a Prussian University; in this he was successful. In Prussia in the 1830s, if one can believe this, one can believe anything! We can be charitable and smile at all this, especially as only recently the collapse of the Soviet Empire has dragged Marxism down to ruins with it.

Collingwood argues in his *Idea of History* that the existence of history creates problems for philosophers which can only be considered and resolved if they adjust their epistemology to the application of historical method. He expresses his admiration for Vico, who, he says, has influenced him more than anybody else. He gives an example of what the study of the history of philosophy entails:

What does X think?

Was he right?

The first question is historical and the second appears philosophical, but really it is only historical. We have to know what problem X had to solve, and we can only know by arguing back from the solution, given of course that the problem can be identified.

If we accept that there is a general process of history how could we best express it? We would state that this takes place as a result of the actions and reactions towards each other, of the different working, professional and ethnic groups of which the society is composed. Actions and reactions are motivated by thought, which expresses itself in language. This establishes a triangle of parity. The shape of this triangle will depend on the pressure of the three components upon each other.

The convergence and divergence of ethnicity is a comparatively recent phenomenon in history, but is slowly yet inexorably altering the shape of the world social infrastructure. We cannot at present tell whether this shape and development will be positive or negative.

Returning to our theme of the relationship between language and history: we will learn more by studying Arabic, than by studying the history of the Arabs.

We immediately discover that the Arabs have no sense of time – they have one tense for both present and future. When the Arab says *aktooboo*, it means both *I write* and *I shall write*. The Arab system for plurals of nouns is extremely complicated and arbitrary, with no simple addition of 's' to singular nouns to make them plural.

Appended below are a few examples to illustrate this point.

Arabic		English	
SINGULAR	PLURAL	SINGULAR	PLURAL
hallasroon	hallakoon	barber	(s)
dooboon	adbaboon	bear	(s)
koorseyoon	karakseyoon	chair	(s)
baboon	abwahboon	door	(s)
sinoon	asnanoon	tooth	teeth
shebakoon	shoobakikoon	window	(s)

Much information may be acquired by examining other languages. If we look at German, we see the phrase:

Kinder	*Kirche*	*Küche*
children	church	kitchen

which prescribes the way of life for women. To add insult to injury Germans sometimes consider women as neuter; they do have a feminine gender also.

Thus	*die Frau*	*das Weib*	*das Fraülein*	*das Mädchen*
	the wife	the wife	the young lady	the girl
	feminine	neuter	neuter	neuter

Imagine the following:

Where is his wife?
It is in the garden.

Where is the young lady?
It is in the kitchen.

In strong antithesis to this degrading attitude to women is the almost fawning attitude towards certain male names. Consider for instance the male name *Herman*. Although this name is not exclusively German, it is however very popular with Germans and if we analyse it, we will easily discover why.

Herman   = Herr man, master
               = masterman

Heer (pronounced as Herr) means army.
Heer man = soldier = master

Another instructive example is the double meaning of *kriegen*:
   =   to fight
   =   to obtain
i.e. one obtains by fighting. This double meaning has become so ingrained that the average German is hardly aware of its existence.

Is it possible to eradicate this entrenched attitude? It appears at first sight to be impossible, or at least highly improbable, but fortunately a powerful remedy is available, as we shall see as we progress through our studies.

If we turn for a moment to Russian we find a word which could only be Russian: *pogrom*. This word means destruction and massacre in general, but in the course of Russian history it is applied only to the massacre of Jews. In 1648 the Ukranian leader Khmielnitsky joined his country with Russia. He subjected many thousands of Jews, men, women and children, to frightful torture and massacre. Russian historians have been indifferent towards these actions. To them Khmielnitsky was a great Russian patriot and they cite him as a model for emulation.

It is reasonable to suppose that Konstantyn Pobedonostev, Procurator of the Holy Synod during the reigns of Alexander II (1856–1881) and Alexander III (1881–1894) did accept this view. He proposed 'a final solution' to the Jewish problem. The Jews themselves were responsible, on account of their Russophobia, for the hatred they aroused. Did not the *Protocols of the Elders of Zion* indicate their lust for world power? Russia was destined by history to bar their road to dominion, and in order to do this it was necessary to take drastic action. The 'final solution' (where have we seen this phrase elsewhere?) would be as follows:

    One third to be exterminated.
    One third to be expelled.
    One third to be converted.

Even Pobedonostev would allow some Jews to live, although his disciple Hitler and the Nazis wanted a world '*Judenrein*' (Jewless).

Reverting for a moment to Khmielnitsky in 1648: this was the year that saw the end of the Thirty Years' War between Catholics and Protestants in Germany. The exhausted combatants agreed that war had not provided a solution to their problem, and that the time had now come for negotiation. It took six months before both sides could agree on the seating arrangements in the hall of the Peace Conference, but finally they found a solution, and hammered out a Treaty – the Treaty of Westphalia 1648, which put an end to the war.

This did not mean, however, that religious persecution ceased in Europe. In France the Huguenot Protestants were still subject to persecution. The Edict of Nantes which had given them freedom was revoked in 1685 by Louis XIV. It is interesting to note that this king was the grandson of King Henry of Navarre, a nominal Protestant who had remarked in 1594 that 'Paris was well worth a mass'.

A lamentable exception proved to be the case in Northern Ireland. There, to Protestants and Catholics alike, the Battle of the Boyne between them seems to have occurred only yesterday, the hatred engendered has been aggravated by the Irish Republican Army (IRA) and continues unabated to this day.

Continuing our method of studying the history of nations through their language we find some interesting examples in Polish. We will not have proceeded very far – in fact, barely scratched the surface – before we encounter some unusual phenomena.

The word *byc* in Polish means 'to be'. The present indicative of this verb is as follows:

Ja jestem	I am
Ty jestes	thou art
On jest	he is
Ona jest	she is
Ono jest	it is
My jestesmy	we are
Wy jestescie	you are
Oni są*	they are

(*pronounce as *sont* in French)

At first sight it is very difficult to see how this has happened; why did the Poles abandon their own wording? It is not a case of borrowing a noun and incorporating it in the language, as we have done with various foreign nouns such as the Russian *samovar*; German *delicatessen, kindergarten, blitz*; French *coup d'état, cul de sac, ménage à trois*; Italian, *la dolce vita, paperazzi*; Yiddish *mazeltov*. Of course, the opposite process is taking place – English words such as cricket, football, rugby etc. have become international.

Resuming the discussion on the Polish word *sq*, there *must* have been a contact at some time which has left a lasting impression on Polish; and by rigorous research, we find this contact in the Polish political system of *elective* monarchy.

This system had been employed for some hundreds of years. When the monarch, male or female (Poland has had queens in the course of its history), died, the Poles invited candidates from European countries to come forward and stake their claim. Before any candidate could be successful, he had to receive the *unanimous* approval of all the members of the Polish Sejm (Parliament). The members were all of the nobility (*szlachta*). If only one member objected, the candidate failed; similarly if this happened Bills in Parliament would fail to be passed.

One can only wonder why this 'system' lasted as long as it did. Obviously it could run into the ground at any time, as soon as Poland's weakness became manifest, to its neighbours, Prussia, Russia, and Austro-Hungary. The French Statesman Mirabeau said in 1789 of Prussia that war was its national industry, and he could have added that it had been so for a long time before that. The rape of Silesia by Frederick the Great of Prussia in 1742 clearly proved the point. Poland's predatory neighbours – Russia, Prussia and Austria – combined to dismember it and the Partitions of 1772–1773 and 1775 sealed its doom.

If we now turn our attention to French, we shall find some interesting facts.

Let us consider for instance the phrase *ménage à trois*. It once meant the cohabitation of one man and two women; the women could be a wife and a mistress or two mistresses and the man would be the master; or one of the women could be the mistress of the *ménage*, and would control its management. In recent years however there has been a sharp alteration in the attitude of the public towards sexual relationships. Today the *ménage* might consist of three homosexuals, three lesbians, two homosexuals and one lesbian or one homosexual and two lesbians. None of these combinations would arouse any outside interest. It is just a fact of life.

Another interesting phrase, *'fille de joie'*, literally a 'girl of joy', but actually meaning 'prostitute', indicates the French attitude to sex, vastly different from the English equivalent 'prostitute'. There are a number of words in English for prostitute – harlot, slag, slut, whore, etc. but how does

English deal with the male equivalent? So ingrained is the term for prostitute that English can only say male prostitute – a prostitute is a woman.

In the same way, we might say: 'The doctor is coming tomorrow.' It is assumed here that the doctor is a man; if it is a woman, we would have to indicate this by saying: 'It is a lady doctor,' as we are so ingrained with the concept that the doctor is a man.

The innate conservatism of the English people is clearly shown by their use of the word 'old'. When they wish to express their satisfaction and pride for X, say, the cry is: 'Good old X!' X may be a boy, young man, or old man; they even express it for women too. If it is old, it is good. Male friends will greet each other using the word 'old' in various ways. 'Hullo, old boy, how are you?' The friend may well reply, 'Fine, old man,' or 'Fine old boy.' Occasionally it may be used in a somewhat disrespectful way: 'My old man [meaning my father] is getting to be a bit of a handful. Is your old man the same?' 'No, old man, my old man is not giving us any trouble at all.'

Another very interesting word is *danegeld* – that is, money exorted by blackmail. More than a thousand years ago, the Vikings of Denmark and Norway were continually raiding England and establishing colonies there. In the year 871 of the Christian Era, there took place the Battle of Ashdown Forest, as a result of which the English paid money to the Danes to prevent further forays. This money was called *danegeld* and led finally to a Viking sitting on the throne of England in the early part of the eleventh century.

A very interesting word in Hebrew is the word *Yoven*. Actually it means 'Greek', but it has acquired an evil meaning through the historical associations between Jews and Greeks. About two thousand years ago, the Greeks conquered Palestine as it then was. Their rule was very oppressive until they were finally driven out by the Jews under the leadership of the Maccabeans. So when Jews speak of the Greeks, this has two meanings:

1. He is a Greek, that is, he is a Greek national.
2. He is a Greek, meaning he is a boor, rough, aggressive, violent.

This could apply to anybody – one Jew could apply this to another Jew, although this is probably the most insulting epithet he could apply. Women in general would not apply this term to each other.

Chapter 2

Giambattista Vico (1668–1744) was a brilliant historical philosopher, the first to see the importance of the relationship between history and language.

Thought is a sign, but not a cause of existence. Philosophy is thought about thought. Mathematics is one of the most certain areas of human knowledge.

Vico saw, for the first time, how philosophy and philology, the one concerned with the universal and eternal, the other with the particular and contingent, could be combined to produce a science of human affairs. He maintained that human customs and beliefs be viewed in the context of particular cities and societies at particular times and places.

Ideas and language are united by nature. Providence makes things operate via causes which work in favour of, rather than against, man's continued existence.

Vico's theory of history is that there is a determinate sequence of stages of development to be followed by every nation, whose development is conditioned solely or primarily by internal factors. He maintained that philology, the study of historical evidence, should be conducted in accordance with the criteria appropriate to a science.

Vico's theory of the poetic nature of early man shows how this affected the development and hence the nature of early institutions and how they would be responsible for the creation of institutions in a non-constitutional context.

The thesis of poetic man carries with it, however, a neat conception of what counts as reality and how to interpret it. Vico does not believe that man cannot be both imaginative and rational at once. He takes reason to be a form of understanding which is abstract, in the same sense that it utilises abstract concepts, whereas the imagination utilises particular images. He maintains that the laws of his own time could have operated in the time of poetic man. He distinguishes three kinds of laws: poetic, heroic and human. Poetic law is customary law, adopted through fear of a god of imaginary origins. Heroic law is a law of formulae, in which the formulae themselves are mistaken for the spirit of the law.

Poetic man's imagination enables him to create an image of God, which supersedes previous beliefs in a plurality of gods. He ascribes to religious belief and laws, the function of serving as a social bond or constraining force, which holds men within social ways, when their normal instinct, which is vicious, would drive them to destroy society.

Vico explains the breakdown of society by a decline in religious belief. Wherever the poetic mind arises, it must be succeeded by the heroic mind.

In history there are two possible makers: historical agents and historians. Each can be thought of as a maker, but what they make does not coincide. The historical agent is the maker of events and institutions whereas the historian is the maker of the history of those events and institutions.

Vico makes a strong analogy between the life of a human being from childhood to old age and that of a nation from infancy to final dissolution.

The historian's own world, and the historian himself, are the product of an historical process, the principles of which leave their trace in his world and therefore in him. The historian can begin to understand history with his understanding of human nature in the historical and social dimensions; he does know this, and it is in virtue of this fact that historical knowledge can transcend mere consciousness and become science.

Chapter 3

Vico observed in his study of Latin that the origins of a great number of words were so scholarly that they seem to have arisen not from common popular usage, but from some inner learning. Latin was full of relatively learned phrases, yet until the time of Pyrrhus (319–272 BC) king of Epirus, the ancient Romans had no pursuits other than agriculture and war. The words were being used without knowledge of their meaning. The Romans derived their religious cults, together with their sacred phrases and pontifical words, from the Etruscans.

Words are symbols of ideas; ideas are symbols and tokens of things. Thought is proper to the human mind, but understanding proper to the divine mind. The human mind participates in reason, but lacks mastery of it. Human truth is what man arranges and makes as he knows it. It is two dimensional, because man grasps only the external of things. Human knowledge is a kind of dissection of the works of nature.

In Latin, *verum* (the true) and *factum* (what is made) are interchangeable.

The sceptic may be conscious that he thinks, but he is ignorant of the causes of thought. Thinking is not the cause of one's being a mind, but a sign of it, and a sign is not a cause.

Useful historians are not those who offer imprecise accounts of facts and general causes, but those who search for the ultimate circumstances of facts and discover particular causes. Man perceives, judges and reasons but his perception is often false, his judgment rash, and his perception defective.

Vico denies the Cartesian concept of knowledge as an essentially private property. He maintains that it is only available to an individual when a society has reached a certain stage of development, i.e. the fully human age, in which concepts proper to the nature of things are available to him only in so far as public knowledge is well founded. It is not essentially private, as Déscartes implied.

The natural law of nations certainly arose with their common customs, and the world has never contained a nation of atheists, since all nations originated in some religion. Aristotle claimed that there is nothing in the intellect which is not present in the senses, but Vico denies this – the mind uses the intellect when, from something which it senses, it gathers something which does not fall under the senses.

Philologists are agreed that being still a human faith, Christianity is older than the fabulous faith of the Greeks.

Sacred history offers a more intelligible description than any gentile history of an original state of nature, or era of families in the beginning, in which fathers ruled under the government of God.

Philosophers all agree, when they discuss the origin of politics, i.e. the origin of the rights which governments possess, that the cities all arose from the state of families.

Because of the two periods of slavery which Jews suffered among the Egyptians and Assyrians, sacred history offers a weightier account of the antiquities of Egypt and Assyria than does Greek history. The first monarch to appear in history is that of Assyria; the first sages, the Chaldeans, also appear there.

The formation of articulate languages in nations which are already founded presents great difficulties and requires much time. It is impossible to understand how a language could express abstract things in terms which are already abstract, unless the language belongs to a nation in which skilled philosophers have existed for a long time. Thus Latin, because it made late contact with the thoughts of Greek philosophy, expresses itself in the sciences, in an impoverished and positively miserable fashion. Yet according to Thucydides, the first truthful and serious historian to write about Greece, the Greeks of his time knew nothing of their own early history, prior to the times of their fathers.

The mind of solitary man, when the occasion of differing human necessities must develop through different states, depends upon the bases of his primary aim of preserving his future, by the preservation first of the family, then of the city, next of the nation, and finally of the whole of mankind. Providence drew impious man from the states of solitude into that of the families, from which the first gentes were born: that is the clans or houses, which later gave rise to the cities.

Reasoning about the natural law of nations must be in accordance with the natural order of ideas. Providence governs the entire natural law of nations.

Vulgar wisdom is a common sense possessed by each people or nation. The concordance of common senses among all peoples is the wisdom of mankind.

Our will is determined by our mind through the power of truth which is what we call conscience. This is because the natural law of the gentes is a law which has arisen with the natural custom of nations, based upon their ideas of their nature. The law of the heroic gentes was based on the principle that the nature of the strong is different and more noble than that of the weak.

A fear of God is called religion. The Oriental Greek and Egyptian gods became the gods common to mankind through wars, alliances and commerce between the nations. In the past, defeated nations gradually disregarded their own defeated gods, lived in fear of the victorious gods, allowed their own language to fall into disuse and came to celebrate the language of the dominant religion.

Mastery of the hieroglyphic language of the first gentes was preserved intact, both among the free peoples of the assemblies and among the monarchs who were restricted to a certain armorial language, a language of coats-of-arms and flags, through which the nations communicated with each other, in wars, alliances, and commerce. This language is the principle of the science of heraldry, as well as that of medals.

The unity of religion united a nation in ancient Rome; the plebeian (*plebs*) were constituted entirely differently in kind from the order of nobles.

The common custom of nations is that their cities should not be divided into religions according to the different gods, for cities divided by religion are either in ruin, or close to it.

The whole body of Roman law provides the most complete and certain public evidence in the whole of gentile antiquity by which we can establish the law of the gentes of Italy, Greece and the other ancient nations.

The Spartans were forbidden any knowledge of letters, so they remained in a state of ferocity; their government remained aristocratic and they retained a great many of the oldest heroic customs of Greece. All philologists agree that there was a ruling order of Herculian races, headed by two kings, elected for life. The Roman government had precisely this form during the period, when only the nobles were literate, and when the state of ferocity endured.

Heroic nature, which lies halfway between the divine and human things of nature, has been largely unknown to us up to now. The communities of men are led naturally to preserve the memory of those customs, laws and orders which hold them fast in their society. If all gentile histories have preserved their fabulous origins, and the Greeks more so than any others, the fables must uniquely contain historical accounts of the oldest customs, orders and laws of the first gentile nations.

When we find fabulous traditions uniform amongst nations far from each other they must have been of ideas, which are naturally common to each other. An example of this is the fable of the heroes, born of the union of gods with mortal women. This fable is common amongst Egyptians, Greeks and Latins, and this gives rise to their heroic ages. Profane history describes the lascivious relationship between gods and women, but sacred history is not contaminated by the slightest taint of paganism, which possibly led the Greeks to name one of their gods Pan, signifying a poetic monster whose nature was part man, and part goat.

Chapter 4

Public medals are the most reliable documents of certain history, so for the period of fabulous and obscure history their place must be taken by various marble remains. These establish the common customs of the first people.

A poverty of conventional language led all the first nations to express themselves by means of objects, which at first must have been natural, and later became carved or painted such as the Egyptian hieroglyphics. Fragments of antiquity, moreover, are everywhere to be found, with characters of carved objects of the same kind as the magical character of the Chaldean.

The Chinese write in hieroglyphics, showing that their origin was not more than four thousand years ago.

When Darius the Persian king sent men to Greece to declare war on them, the Greeks replied in hieroglyphics. The science of these characters was concealed by the priests. Nothing in nature precludes the existence of giants: such indeed were the ancient Germans, who retained a large measure of their most ancient origins, both in custom and language, because they never allowed any civilised nations to exercise control, within their (German) boundaries.

Universal profane history is connected with sacred history by means of the start of Greek history, the source of all we know about it.

Chaos must first have meant the confusion of human seed and then that of the seed of the whole of nature.

Amongst Egyptians, Greeks and Romans it was born identically, based upon observation of thunderbolts and eagles, the weapons and birds of love. This is why the Romans retained eagles on top of their sceptres, why the Greeks retained wings on Mercury's sceptre and why both Greeks and Romans kept carved or painted eagles among their military insignia.

False religions cannot have arisen other than from the idea of a body of strength and power superior to anything human which, because they were by nature ignorant of causes, men imagined as possessing intelligence. This is the origin of idolatry. The natural curiosity of men awakes in them a desire to know the significance of anything unusual in nature. This is the universal origin of the whole of divination. When man is ignorant, he judges what he does not know in accordance with his own nature. Idolatry and divination are the inventions of an entirely imaginative poetry. This is the universal origin of sacrifice amongst all the gentiles who procured or sought the auspices superstitiously in their ceremonies.

Fables and true speech meant the same thing, and constituted the vocabulary of the first nations.

A poverty of words naturally makes men sublime in expression, serious in conception and acute in understanding much in brevity, which are the three supreme virtues of language. It reveals further the origin of the brevity and seriousness of ancient laws, such as the Law of the twelve tables, for this was committed to writing when the Romans were still in extremely barbaric times. It also reveals the acuteness of Florentine aphorisms, which were born in the Old Market in Florence in the most barbaric of Italian eras from the ninth to the twelfth centuries.

The three most important virtues of poetic language are that it should heighten and expand our powers of imagination, that it should give brief expression to the ultimate circumstances by which things are defined and that it should transport the mind to the most remote things and present them in a captivating manner as though decked out in ribbon. An absence or scarcity of reasoning brings with it a strength of the senses, which in turn leads to vividness and the imagination, and a vivid imagination is the best painter of the images, which objects impress on the senses. Poetry was the first common language of all ancient nations including the Hebrews.

Since words are articulated human sounds and children are led naturally to express things by imitation of these sounds the majority of words in all languages owe their origin to onomatopoeic monosyllables of this sort. Jove, the first of all gods, was called Zeus by the Greeks after the hiss of a thunderbolt.

As inland nations arose first everywhere, to be followed by maritime nations, words of indisputable foreign origin must be secondary words, introduced after nations came to know one another upon the occasion of wars, alliance and commerce.

Proverbs are observed under different aspects by different nations. Thus some cities of Hungary are called one thing by the Hungarians, another by the Germans, and yet another by the Turks, using words which sound different in each case, by shouts, grunts, and murmurs, doing so only under the impulse of the most violent passions.

The Greeks, in their time of superstition, regarded those who made discoveries useful to mankind as having a divine aspect, and in this way, created their imaginary gods.

Men are led naturally to revere providence, and that providence alone must therefore have founded and ordered the nations. By means of the first fable, the first ignorant men of the gentile world taught themselves a curt theology, which included idolatry and divination.

In the Hebrew language, although it is wholly poetic and surpasses in sublimity that of Homer himself (a fact recognised even by philologists), one finds not a single mention of polytheism. This itself must be a demonstration that the fathers of sacred history really existed during the many centuries which it recounts.

Poets who meant their fables to be true narrations of the things of their own times, are the real mythologists. No tradition can be created, however fabulous, which did not originally have some basis of truth.

Plato, in founding republics which could not be put into practice, lost sight of providence. He also believed in the possibility of a republic of sages, whose women were held in common.

The original words which the Latins uttered must all at first have been monosyllables in which the origins of native languages must everywhere be found.

Since words are articulated a dictionary consists of mental words, common to all nations, by expressing the uniform ideas of substance, through which the nations thought about the same human necessities, or that which is common to all, but looking at them through differing properties, according to their diversities of place, climate, nature, and custom. The dictionary narrates the origins of the different vital languages, all of which share a common ideal language.

The fathers, in the state of the families, and in that of the cities to which they gave rise, had certain properties:

1. Imagination of deities.
2. Begetting children by women, under certain divine auspices.
3. Of heroic or Herculian origin.
4. Possessing of the science of the auspices.
5. For the sacrifices they made in their houses.
6. For their unlimited power over their families.

7. For the strength with which they killed wild animals, cultivated the wild land, and defended their fields.
8. For the magnanimity, allowing violent men in the state of bestial communion to take refuge in their asylums.
9. For the high repute which their capacity to crush the violent and support the weak brought them.
10. For the sovereign dominion of their fields, acquired naturally.
11. For their sovereign powers of arms, which accompanied sovereign dominion of the fields.
12. For their sovereign choice of law, and of punishments, which accompanied sovereign power of arms.

The Hebrews called the fathers Levites from *el*, which means 'strong'. The Assyrians called them Chaldeans or wise men, the Persians magi or diviners, and the Egyptians, priests.

The first civil governments were born in the form of aristocracies. In Latin *ver* denotes a man of civil power and *homo* denotes a man of ordinary nature, obligated to follow others, who have the right to lead.

Chapter 5

Everything which pertains to philology is governed with certain and determinate meanings by philosophy.
 The stages of utility are as follows: first, the necessity that states should worship a provident god; next, the certainty of clans by solemn marriage; finally the necessity of the distinction of terrestrial domain through burial of the dead. This constitutes the common sense of the whole of mankind, which will prevent them from relapsing into the state of bestial freedom.
 The rule for judging the state of nations should be whether the people are drawn closer together or driven further apart. The Platonists concur with all legislators on these points. Divine providence must exist. Human passions should be moderated and human virtues made from them; and human souls must be immortal.
 Philosophy considers man as he ought to be, and this can only profit the very few who wish to live in the Republic of Plato, and not wallow in the filth of Romulus, fabled creator of the City of Rome, together with his brother Remus.
 To the three vices prevalent in the whole of mankind, violence, avarice and ambition, legislation creates the army, commerce and the court, and thus from these vices, it creates civil happiness.
 Philosophy contemplates reason, whence comes knowledge of the true philology which observes the authorities of human will, whence comes consciousness of the certain. Philologists include grammarians, historians and critics engaged in cognition of the languages and affairs of peoples. Philosophers, who failed to ascertain their reasoning with the authority of the philologists, fell halfway short in their task, as did the philologists, who failed to verify their authority with the reasoning of the philosophers.

Human will, by its nature most uncertain, is made certain and determined by the common sense of men, concerning human necessities and utilities.

Uniform ideas born among whole peoples, ignorant of one another, must have a common basis of truth.

The natural law of the gentes was born independently in nations, without their knowing anything of one another, but later, as a result of wars, embassies, alliances and commerce, it was common to the whole of mankind.

Vulgar traditions must have had a public basis of truth whence they were born and maintained by whole peoples over long stretches of time. Expressions of the vulgar must be important witnesses of the ancient customs practised by the peoples at the time when the languages were formed. Where an ancient language has maintained the autonomy until it has reached its fruition, its language must be a great witness of the customs of the world's first times.

While the Greeks had expressed their things in heroic language, the Romans expressed theirs in the language of the vulgar. Proverbs are maxims of vulgar wisdom, perceived as identical substance by all nations, but expressed under as many different aspects as there are nations.

Sacred history is older than any of the most ancient profane histories. It recounts for a long period, of more than eight hundred years, the state of nature under the patriarchs, the state of the families upon which the peoples and cities later arose. The Hebrews have preserved their memories with great clarity. Their religion was founded by God, by the prohibition of the practice of divination in which the gentile nations all arose. The whole world of ancient nations divided itself into Hebrews and Gentiles.

However, two great fragments of Egyptian antiquity have come down to us. One is, that the Egyptians divided the whole of the world's past prior to then, into three ages: those of the gods, of the heroes, and of men. Through these three ages, three languages had been spoken correspondingly. These were the hierglyphic or sacred language, the symbolic or heroic language, and the alphabetic or vulgar language of men.

In his poems, Homer refers to a language older than his own and calls it the language of the gods.

The world of peoples began everywhere with religion. Where peoples have grown wild through arms, so that human laws no longer obtain among them, religion provides the only effective means of subduing them.

Where the human mind sinks itself into ignorance, it makes itself the measure of the universe in respect of everything it does not know. Wonder is the daughter of ignorance. The power of the imagination is proportionate to the weakness of the capacity to reason.

Fear produced the first gods of the world; false religions arose not by deception by others, but by man's own credulity. Every gentile nation had a Jove, who struck through thunderbolts.

All barbaric histories have their fabulous origins. Fables are ideal truths, conforming to the merits of those of whom the vulgar create them and are false in fact, only to the degree that they fail to give credit to those who are worthy of it. Poetic truth is a form of metaphysical truth in comparison with which any physical truth which fails to conform must be false. In its childhood, the world consisted of poetic nations since poetry is nothing but imitation. Arts are nothing but imitations of nature, and in a certain sense real poems. Poetic judgments are formed to a sense of passion and feeling, in contrast to philosophical judgments which are formed by reflection involving reasoning.

The fables which arose amongst the first savage and primitive men were wholly severe, conforming to the foundation of nations emerging from a ferocious and bestial liberty. With the passing of time, and changes of custom, they were altered, observed, and made inappropriate in dissolute and corrupt times – even earlier than Homer. Religion mattered to the Greeks and, not wishing that the gods be opposed to their prayers, as they were to their customs, they ascribed the latter to the gods, and gave lewd, indecent, and the most obscene senses to their fables.

The first theology of the Egyptians was merely history dressed up in fables, for which their descendants began to invent mystical meanings.

The first authors among the Orientals, Egyptians, Greeks and Latins and the first writers in the new European languages, were poets. The poetic idiom, involving images, likenesses, comparisons and natural properties, must have been subsequent to this natural speech.

Men express their deep emotions by breaking into song, as is shown by those in extremities of grief or joy. The first authors of the gentile nations must have formed their first languages by singing.

Language must have begun with monosyllabic words, just as amid the present wealth of articulate words in which they are now born, children begin with such words.

Ideas and languages must have kept in step as they gathered pace.

Chapter 6

The human mind is inclined naturally to see itself through the senses outwardly in the body, and with great difficulty to understand itself by means of reflection.

The universal principle of etymology in all languages is that words are transferred from bodies, and bodily properties, to signify the things of mind and spirit.

The order of ideas must proceed according to the order of things. The order of human things proceeded in the following manner: first there were forests, then isolated dwellings, whence villages, next cities, and finally, states. A great principle of etymology is that the histories of words of native languages be recorded in accordance with this series of human things. We can see this in Latin where nearly the whole body of words are of rural and agricultural origin.

The first to arise in mankind are the huge and clumsy; then the magnanimous and proud; next the valiant; and just nearer to us come the impressive figures, with great shows of virtue accompanying great vices, who won a reputation for true glory among the vulgar. These include Alexander the Great and Julius Caesar. Later still came the sad reflective type, such as Tiberius; and finally the violent, dissolute, and brazen such as the Roman emperors, Caligula, Nero and Domitian. The first type was necessary in order to subject man to man in the state of the families, and to dispose him to obedience, to the laws of the state of the cities yet to come; the second type, who naturally did not give way to his equals, was necessary in order to establish the aristocratic form of state on the basis of the families; the third was necessary in order to open the way to popular liberty; the fourth was necessary for the introduction of monarchies; the fifth was necessary to consolidate them, and the sixth to overthrow them.

All this provides a part of the principles of the ideal eternal history, traversed in time by all nations, in their birth, growth, perfection, decline and fall. Native customs, and those of natural liberty, above all, do not all change at once, but by degrees and over a long time.

All nations originated in the cult of some divinity in the state of the families; the fathers must have been the sages in the divinity of auspices, the priests who made sacrifices to procure them, to understand them properly, and the kings who brought divine laws to their families.

There is a vulgar tradition that the first to govern in the world were kings, another one that the most worthy by nature, were created the first kings. There is a further vulgar tradition, that the first kings were sages. Plato established this statement by his observation that philosophers should be kings, and kings philosophers.

In the persons of the first families, wisdom, priesthood and sovereignty were united, and sovereignty and priesthood were dependencies of wisdom.

There is a vulgar tradition that the first form of government in the world was the monarchic state. It is characteristic of the strong, not to lose by indolence what they have gained through strength, but through necessity or utility, to relinquish a little at a time, and to the least extent possible.

The heroic kingdoms were those in which kings administered the law at home, directed wars abroad and were the heads of religion. The Roman kings were sovereign in sacred things, being named *rem reges sacrorum* (kings of the sacred rites). Ancient states had no laws for the punishment of private offences and the correction of private wrongs, because they had not yet been domesticated by means of laws, and as a result duels and reprisals took place. Ancient Roman history shows up the proud, avaricious and cruel habits of the nobles over the plebeians. For a long time they drove the plebeians to serve them in war without pay, and drowned them in a sea of usury. When the plebeians could not pay they were incarcerated in prisons and beaten with switches across their naked shoulders.

People will behave heroically in war, if in peace time they take part in contests for honour. The nobles naturally devoted themselves to the safety of their country, through which they held all civil honour, safe within their order.

The weak desire law; the powerful decline to accept it; the princes protect the weak. Starting with Augustus, a Roman leader created innumerable laws pertaining to private justice. Throughout Europe, sovereigns and powers accepted into their monarchies and free states the corpus of Roman civil law and that of canon law.

Natural liberty is more ferocious the more that goods attach to the necessities of the body itself, whilst civil servitude is anchored in goods of fortune not necessary to life.

Men wish to escape from subjection and they yearn for equality, so that in the aristocratic states, the plebeians transformed them into popular states. Then men strove to overcome their equals, and the popular states became corrupted into states of the powerful. Then they wished to set others beneath them. From this emerged the popular state, the worst of all tyrannies in which there are as many tyrants as there are audacious and dissolute men in the cities. At this point the plebeians turn to the shelter of monarchies to find a remedy.

Men at first lived in the mountains, then later descended to the plains, and finally had confidence enough to venture to the shores of the sea. Inland nations were founded first, and maritime nations later. The Hebrew people, founded in Mesopotamia, the most inland area of the first habitable world, were the oldest of all nations. The first monarchy, that of the Assyrians over the Chaldean people, was founded there; the Chaldeans produced Zoroaster who was the foremost of the first sages in the world.

Nations in their barbarism are impenetrable, and must be entered forcibly by war from outside, or opened naturally for the benefit of commerce from within. In this way did Psammetichus open Egypt to the Greeks of Ionia and Caria, who after the Phoenicians must have been famous for maritime trade. In this way the temple of Samian Juno was founded in Ionia, and the mausoleum of Artemis built in Caria. These were two of the seven wonders of the world. Fame in maritime trade settled finally upon the people of Rhodes who erected the great Colossus of the Sun, in the entrance of their port.

There is a further etymology for words of certain foreign origins which is different from the etymology for native words. Thus Naples was first named with a Syrian word Sirena which shows that the Syrians were the first to lead a colony there for reasons of trade. Later it was called Parthenope, which is a heroic Greek word and finally, in vulgar Greek, Naples. These names prove that the Greeks later went there to open up trade, and in this way, a language composed of a mixture of Phoenician and Greek must have developed there.

In exactly the same way a Syrian colony, called Sirls, existed on the shores of Taranto, the inhabitants of which were called Sirites. The

Greeks later named this colony Poleion, from which Minerva Polias, whose temple was there, took her name.

There is nothing however which gives more pleasure than the celebration of natural custom. It follows therefore that human nature is sociable. Man is not unjust by nature in the absolute, but fallen by weak nature. Men cannot exist without the principle of free will, in which all religions concur.

The Roman jurists defined the natural law of the gentes as a law ordained by divine providence. There is a difference between the natural law of the Hebrew and those of the gentes and the philosophers. The gentes received only ordinary aids from providence but the Hebrews received in addition extraordinary aids from God. As a result they divided the whole world of nations into Hebrews and Gentiles. The philosophers, who did not arise until some two thousand years after the founding of the gentes, represent their natural law more perfectly in their reasoning than do the gentes in their customs.

Doctrines must begin with the times in which their subject matters begin. The gods were divided as follows: the greater gentes consecrated by the familiar prior to the cities. They emerge as a generation of gods created naturally in the minds of the Greeks in the following order: Jove, Juno, Diana, Apollo, Vulcan, Saturn, Vesta, Mars, Venus, Minerva, Mercury and Neptune – twelve. Mankind began in all the first nations in the time of the families under gods of the greater gentes.

For intelligent men the law is whatever the principle of equal utility in cases dictates.

The true in the law is a certain light and brilliance of natural reason, which shines forth in them.

The natural equity of fully developed human reason is a practice of wisdom in matters of utility, since wisdom in its fullness is nothing but the science of making that use of things which belongs to them by nature. This constitutes the principle of benign law, regulated by the natural equity which belongs naturally to civilised nations. The civil world itself has certainly been made by man, and its principles therefore must be rediscovered within the modifications of our human mind.

Philosophers have all earnestly endeavoured to attain knowledge of the natural world, and have neglected to meditate upon this world of nations or civil world, knowledge of which, since men had made it, they could attain. This result originated in that shortcomings of the human mind were immersed and buried in the body. It was naturally inclined to have a sense of bodily things, but required very much effort and work to understand itself, like the physical eye, which sees all objects external to itself, but needs a mirror to see itself.

All nations, barbaric or human, preserve three human customs: they all have a religion, contract solemn marriages, and bury their dead. No human actions are celebrated with more revered ceremonial and more sanctified solemnity than religion, marriage and burials. Uniform ideas born among peoples ignorant of one another must have a common basis of truth.

All nations believe in a provident divinity, whence only four primary religions have been possible throughout all the times and places of this civil world:

a. The Hebrews
b. The Christians
c. The gentiles who believe in the divinity of several gods, each thought to be composed of a body and free mind.
d. Lastly are the Mohammedans who believe in the divinity of a God who is an infinite mind in an infinite body, since they expect pleasures of the senses, as their reward in the after life.

No nation has believed in a god who is wholly body, nor in a god who is wholly a mind, but who is not free.

All gentile nations have concurred in the view that the souls of the unburied remain restlessly on earth, wandering around their unburied bodies, and hence, that they do not die with their bodies but are immortal.

The terrifying thought of some divinity is the only effective means of restoring to duty a liberty-run world. Men, no matter how wild, fierce and horrifying they be, are not devoid of some notion of God. When man has fallen into despair of all nature's help, he desires something superior to save him. Superior to nature is God, and this is the light which God has shone upon all men. There is a common human custom that as they grow old, and feel the lack of their natural forces, libertines naturally become religious.

Because their nature is corrupt men are tyrannised by self love when they pursue first and foremost only what is useful to them, and do nothing for their fellows. They are unable to subdue their passions and direct themselves to justice. Although man is unable to achieve all he desires, he may expect to achieve all the utilities which he needs, and this is called just. Hence it is divine justice which regulates the whole of human justice and preserves human society.

Metaphysics must begin with the times in which the first man began to think humanly, and not with those when philosophers began to reflect upon human ideas.

Men were for long incapable of grasping the true end of reason, which is the source of that inner justice, which satisfies the intellect.

Our mythologies, which are not forced and distorted but simple and natural, are the civil liberties of the first peoples who are found everywhere naturally to have been poets. The etymologies of native languages which give the histories of the things which words signify are in accordance with the order of ideas which is the basis upon which the history of languages must proceed.

We develop the mental vocabularies of those human sociable things whose identity of substance is felt by all nations, though they express them diversely in language because of their modifications.

The true is sifted from the false in everything, which over the long course of centuries has been preserved by vulgar traditions which having themselves been preserved for such a long time, and by entire peoples, must have had a public basis of truth.

Great fragments of antiquity afford great illumination, when cleansed, reassembled and restored to their proper places.

The basic method of philosophising is to think and see the philological one, which follows it. Thus can their authority be confirmed by reason, and reason is confirmed by their authority.

Whatever is sensed as just by all or by the majority of men, must be the rule of sociable life, and is consistent both with the vulgar wisdom of all the legislators and with the wisdom of the philosophers. These must constitute the limits of human reason, and it would be folly to try to go beyond this.

Chapter 7

Human nature carries with it the senses which are the only means whereby it knows things.

Thus poetic wisdom, the first wisdom of the gentile world, must have had a metaphysics which was not rational and abstract but sensed and imagined, as that of the first man, devoid of reason and wholly composed of powerful senses, and vigorous imaginations. Poetry originated in these people as a divine poetry, because it arose at a time in which they imagined that the causes of the things which they were sensing and admiring were gods. This is similar to what we see today with children who hold inanimate things in their hands, playing and talking with them as if they were living people.

Great poetry must invent sublime fables, befitting the popular understanding, perturb to excess the very man, in order to attain its end, to teach the vulgar to act virtuously as the poets taught them to do.

The first men of robust bodily strength gave expression to their violent passions by howls and grunts; when they heard the whistle of bolts and the roar of thunder in the sky, they imagined that this was due to a god, and they named him Jove, the first god of the so-called greater gentes. In this way they began to celebrate their natural curiosity, daughter of ignorance and mother of knowledge, which gives birth to wonder. They turned the whole of nature into a vast animate body with passions and feelings.

The first theological poets invented for themselves the first divine fable – the greatest of all they were later to invent –that of Jove, king and father of men and gods, in the act, moreover, of hurling bolts of thunder and lightning. The very poets who invented Jove came to believe in him, and, through terrifying religions, feared, revered and worshipped him. Thus the first men who spoke in signs, believed that thunder and lightning were Jove's signs – these signs were real words and that nature was Jove's language.

The gentes believed that divination was the science of this language, which the Greeks called theology, meaning the science of the speech of the gods. Jove received the title of *soter* or saviour because he did not strike down men with his bolts and he also put a stop to the wanderings of the giants, as a result of which they later became the sovereigns of the gentes.

Every nation had a Jove. The Egyptians claimed that their Jove, Amnon, was the oldest god. The theological poets were thought to be sages who understood the language of the gods, as conceived through Jove's auspices, and who were designated divine, in the sense of diviners, or the sense that they could predict.

The Greek poets were called *mystae*, a word which Homer translates as 'the interpreters of the gods', for they explained the divine mysteries of the auspices and oracles. Oracles and sybils are the most ancient things of the gentile world. The first people, simple and rough, invented the gods, from their fear of present power. The origin of idolatry provides a demonstration of that of divination, for they shared a single birth. This was followed by the sacrifices which men made to procure the auspices. In this way the poets founded religion among the gentiles.

Chapter 8

The first authority which arose was divine; the authority drove the giants of those days underground to the bottom of the caves within the mountains, and there concealed them. When Jove wants to prove that he is king of gods and men, Greek fable asserts that if all gods and men were to hold on to a chain at one end he alone would drag them along behind him.

The divine authority was followed by human authority in the full philosophical sense of a property of human nature, which cannot be taken from man without destroying him. Virtue cannot be deprived of its victory by envy. This authority resides in the free use of the will – intellect is in a passive capacity, which is subservient to the truth, for this is the point of departure of everything human. The authority of human nature was followed by that of natural law.

During the period of the first thunderbolts, men, by occupying and for long remaining in the lands where they were, became lords of those lands by occupation and long possession, which is the source of all ownership in the world. These gentes were the ancient noble houses which, when they had ramified into many families, composed the first kingdoms and cities.

Human will is by its nature most uncertain with regard to the things of the obscure distant past of nations; thus the philosophy of authority reduces philology to the form of a science.

The first Muse began with Jove's thunderbolts. Homer defines it as knowledge of good and evil; philosophers found it easy to interpose their maxim, that the origins of wisdom must lie in piety. This first Muse must have been Urana, who contemplates the sky in search of auguries, and who has come to represent astronomy.

The Roman jurists have posited divine providence as their principle. Their reasoning was concerned with the natural law of the gentes, and not that of philosophers as moral theologians.

Starting from the first age of the world, the Greek poets have faithfully told us in their fables of the flood and the existence of beings who were giants by nature, thus providing a true narration of the origins of profane history, but their successors were unable to enter into the imagination of the first founders of the gentile world, which had led them to believe that they were seeing gods. The first impious giants did not wage war against the gods. They had no notion of them, until Jove was hurling his bolts of thunder and lightning. The sky was for them the peak of the mountains.

The fable of the heaping of a number of mountains upon one another must have been invented after its presence in the Odyssey foisted on him by others, for in his time it was sufficient that Olympus alone should shake in order to bring about the fall of the gods; in the Illiad, Homer always describes the gods as living solely on the top of Mount Olympus.

Chapter 9

Metaphysics contemplates things in all the categories of being, and is also logic, as a result of considering them in all the categories of signification. Poetry is a poetic metaphysics through which the poets imagined bodies for the most part to be divine substances; the same poetry can be considered as poetic logic, through which it signifies things. Logic derives from the word *logos*, which first meant 'fable' and became the Italian *favella* (language). The Greeks also used the word *mythos* for fable, from which the Latins derived *mutue* (mute). Thus in the mute era was born the mental language which, according to Strabo, existed before vocal or articulated language from which *logos* signifies both idea and word.

It is of greater importance to religion that one should meditate on it rather than that one should speak it. So the first language in the first mute age of the nations must have commenced with signs or actions of objects which were naturally related to their ideas, and for this reason *logos* or *verbum* meant 'deed' to the Hebrews and 'thing' to the Greeks. The first language, that of the theological poets, was not a language which accorded with the nature of things.

The first men understood Jove, Cybele and Neptune to be substances of the sky, earth and sea, which they considered to be animate divinities, and believed to be gods.

When man wishes to draw forth spiritual things from his understanding, he requires the assistance of imagination to enable him to express them and, like painters, create human images for them. The theological poets gave sense and passion to bodies even as vast as the sky, earth and sea.

Later, with the diminution of these vast fantasies and the strengthening of abstractions, the former were taken as miniature signs of the latter.

Babel Erased 33

Thus Jove became so small and light that he is carried in flight by an eagle. Neptune rides over the sea in a frail chariot and Cybele is seated on a lion.

The mythologies must have been the proper language of the fables and must have been allegories proper to them. These allegories signify the different species or individuals in general. They must have a univocal meeting, comprised of a quality common to their species.

All metaphors come to signify the labours of abstract minds, and must belong to times in which philosophies had begun to become more refined. In all languages, the words necessary to cultivate arts and science have rural origins.

In all languages the greater part of expressions concerning inanimate things are created by metaphors drawn from the human body and its parts, and from the human senses and passions: for example, 'head' for summit or beginning; 'mouth' for every sort of hole; 'lip' for the rim of a vase; the 'teeth' of a plough or rake; a 'tongue' of sea; a 'neck' of land; and the 'arms' of a river. When man is ignorant he makes himself the measure of the universe.

Rational metaphysics teaches that man becomes everything through understanding by which man unfolds his mind. The first poets were unable to abstract forms and qualities from their subjects, whilst many miniature fables are examples of the metonymy of cause for effect in which the causes are imagined as women clad in the effects of these causes, such as ugly poverty and old age, and called 'death'. Synecdoche is a figure of speech in which a part is substituted for a whole, or a whole for a part, hence the army, for a soldier. It next passed into metaphor by the raising of particulars to universals, or by some parts with other parts, which go to make up their whole. 'Head' was used for man or person in vulgar Latin, because in the dense woods, only a man's head could be seen from a distance, for 'man' itself is an abstract word which comprehends the body and all bodily parts, the mind and all mental faculties, the spirit and all its propensities. In the early days in Latin, *tectum* stood for the whole house, because coverings sufficed for houses. In the same way *puppis* (rook) stood for ship because, being high, it is the first part to be seen by land-dwellers; for the same reason, in the recurrence of barbarism, they used 'sail' for ship. Thus also *macro* (point) for sword, for it was the point which men felt and which caused their fear.

It took many centuries for the astronomical word 'year' to arise among the nations, and in the Florentine countryside, they still talk of harvesting so many times to indicate so many years.

Irony could only have begun in the age of reflection for it is formed from falsehood, by dint of a reflection which borrows a mask of truth. Since the first men of the gentile world were as simple as children, who are truthful by nature, the first fables could have represented nothing through falsehood, so they must have been true narrations.

Metamorphosis was created by the division of ideas. For just as the inner regions of the earth support a farm on the soil, and whatever is sown, planted, or built on it, so a transformation of ideas is effected by a person's support of an act of which he approves.

Poetic language, by dint of its poetic characters, leads to many important discoveries relating to ancient times. Thus Solon must have been someone rich in vulgar wisdom, leader of the plebes in those early times, when Athens was an aristocratic state. The heroes or nobles, believing that a certain nature of theirs was of divine origin, claimed the gods, and their auspices, as their own. They conceded to the plebs who were held to be of bestial origin by the customs of natural liberty. Solon urged the plebs to consider themselves as equals with the nobles, and said they ought to be equal with them in law. The Roman plebs began to achieve equality of civil liberty with the patricians, until the form of the Roman State was completely changed from aristocratic to popular.

This example was followed by the plebs of the peoples; universally they changed aristocratic states into popular ones. Solon's famous phrase *nosce le elsum* (know thyself) was inscribed in all the public places of the city. The Athenians ascribed to Solon all their laws, just as the Egyptians ascribed everything they found useful in human civil life to Hermes Trismegistus.

Similarly all laws concerning the orders were attributed to Romulus; to Numa, all laws concerning sacred things and divine ceremonies of which in its most sumptuous times, the Roman religion later made great show; and to Servius Tullius, the census which is the basis of democratic states and a large number of other laws to do with popular liberty.

By means of this census the plebs won from the nobles ownership of the fields; the tribunes of the plebs were later created for the defence of this part of their natural liberty, and the tribunes subsequently led them, step by step, to attain a full civil liberty.

To Tarquinius Priscus, went all the insignia and emblems with which, in its most brilliant times, the majesty of the Roman empire later glittered.

The law of quiritary ownership which the nobles communicated to the plebs was the first law to be written on a public tablet. The plebs were known as the *socii* of the heroic cities, partaking of the labours and dangers of wars, but not of the spoils and gains.

Aesop was made a poetic character, and when he was made the first moral philosopher, he gave his directions through fables, just as Solon became the sage who established the free Athenian state with his laws.

Chapter 10

There are very many theories concering the origin of languages and letters, contradictory and confusing, and it is very difficult to get at the root of it. Because of this inherent difficulty some scholars claim that they are of divine invention.

They all thought the origin of letters to be a thing apart from that of language, though the two were connected by nature, though they should have been *united* by the words 'grammar' and 'character'. Grammar is defined as 'the art of speaking' and letters are *grammata* so that grammar should be defined as the art of writing, as in truth it first was. The nations, being at first mute, all spoke in writing.

The first men conceived the idea of things through imaginative characters; being mute, these men expressed themselves by actions and objects, which have natural relationships with these ideas, and thus expressed themselves in a language of natural meaning, which according to Plato and Iamblichus was at one time spoken on earth.

Scholars have treated the origins of languages and letters separately, whereas by nature they are connected.

The Egyptians asserted that in the whole previous duration of their world three languages had been spoken, corresponding in number and order to three ages, which had elapsed in that world: the ages of the gods, of the heroes and of men. The first had been hieroglyphic or divine, the second had been symbolic, in signs of heroic coats-of-arms, and the third had been alphabetic, in order that the needs of daily life might be communicated among men distant from one another.

The early gentile nations were originally without speech, so they must have expressed themselves by means of actions or bodies which bore natural relations to their ideas; second that they must have ensured the limits of their farms and kept continuous testimony of their rights by means of signs; and third, that they all used arms.

Tacitus notes that the ancient Germans lacked the secrets of letters, so that they were unable to write their hieroglyphics, which lasted until the times of Rudolph of Austria (11th to 12th centuries), when official documents began to be written in a vulgar German script. In northern France a hieroglyphic speech called rebus the Picardie existed, which, as in Germany, must have been a speech by means of hieroglyphics, which the Chinese use to this very day.

The Greeks had 30,000 gods for they made a deity of every stone, spring or stream, plant or crag, just as American Indians made a god of everything which surpassed their slight understanding. The divine fables of Latin and Greek must have been the true first hieroglyphics, or sacred and divine characters, corresponding to those of the Egyptians.

The second language, which correspond to the age of the heroes, was described by the Egyptians as a language spoken in symbols. These must have consisted in the metaphors, images, likenesses and comparisons, which an articulate language was later to create into the whole ornamentation of poetic speech.

In the recurrence of barbarism in Europe, when various languages were reborn, the first language of the Spaniards was that called El Romance, and therefore was that of heroic poetry. In France, the first to write in vulgar French was Arnaut Daniel Pacca. The first writers in Italy were the Florentine and Sicilian composers of rhyme.

The alphabetic language of the Egyptians, a language necessary for expressing the needs of common daily life used by people living at a distance from one another, must have been used by the vulgar class of a sovereign race of Egypt which must have been that of Thebes, whose king Ramses spread his authority over the whole of that great nation; among the Egyptians, this language corresponds to the age of 'men', the name given to the plebs of the heroic people, to distinguish them from the heroes.

Vulgar speech and writing are the right of people. Thus when the Emperor Claudius invented three new letters, which Latin needed, the Romans were not willing to accept them.

The resemblance between vulgar words in Egyptian and Phoenician was so striking, that one of the nations must have received them from the other. The Phoenicians, who were actually the earliest nation in the world as merchants, took their vulgar letters into Egypt when they traded there, and into Greece also. The hieroglyphics they employed, they had received from the Chaldeans, who were the earliest mathematicians and astronomers in the world. Their prophet Zoroaster's name means 'observer of the stars' and he was the first sage of the gentile world.

The naming of letters with compound sounds was a late introduction among the Greeks. When the latter came to Egypt, they named the capital of that country Thebes, because it resembled in some respects their own native Thebes.

Herodotus, the father of Greek history, wrote in vulgar language. As the heroic or poetic language was founded by the heroes, so the vulgar languages were introduced by the vulgar, who were the plebs of the heroic people, whose languages were properly called *vernacular* by the Latins, although they could not have been introduced by those Vernae whom the grammarians define as 'slaves bred at home, of slaves in war' for these naturally acquire the languages of the nations in which they are born.

Metaphor creates the major corpus of language in all nations.

A difficult problem to resolve is why there are so many diverse vulgar languages. Differences in climate are certainly a very important factor. They have led people to consider the same utilities or necessities of human life under different aspects, thus engendering national customs, which are in general different, and at times conflicting, so that in this way, there have arisen as many different languages, as there are different nations. This is shown clearly by proverbs, which are maxims of human life, which are the same in substance, but expressed in accordance with as many different aspects as there are, and have been, nations. Thus one finds that the same things which are named one way in sacred history, have different names in profane history.

Today things are still given different names by different people. Thus the cities of Hungary are each given different names by the Hungarians, Greeks, Germans and Turks.

In German, a living heroic language, almost all names of foreign extraction are transformed into its own native names.

Since gods, heroes and men all commenced in the same time, so did their languages. That of the gods was almost wholly mute and only very slightly articulate; that of the heroes, was a language in which the mute and articulate were mixed in equal degree, as were expressions of the vulgar and heroic characters in which the heroes wrote; and that of man was a language almost wholly articulate.

Chapter 11

The Transmissibility of Language

It is very clear from Vico's writing that he was strongly in favour of the transmissibility of language and that he also favoured the incorporation into a nation's language of phrases and sentences originally from another language. Let us take an example of English and French, the expression '*coup d'état*'. This originated in French but has now become incorporated into English and is part of the English language. This transmissibility of language is part of a universal linguistic interflow and all languages are enriched by it.

Vico's ideas of the transmissibility of language received a tremendous fillip following Sir William Jones' discovery of Sanskrit. Sir William was an outstanding eighteenth-century linguist who, during the course of his work as a judge in India, discovered Sanskrit and realised that elements of many languages, both eastern and western, derived from Sanskrit. Vico would, indeed, have been exhilarated to find his theories corroborated by Sir William and that his ideas of the transmissibility of language were thus vindicated.

We are now able to study several examples of the accuracy of Vico's ideas.

Vico, the brilliant Italian historical philosopher who lived in the eighteenth century, was the first to realise the importance and significance of the relationship between language and history. He considered that the historian's duty was to approach his task by using scientific methods. As human knowledge is inevitably limited, one cannot overstep the boundaries, and one must understand that nothing can be known unless it already exists; and knowledge of it depends on knowing how it has been created.

History, which obviously is something made by the human mind, is thus an object of human knowledge. There is no antithesis, in regard to the Italian language, between what it is and what the people who use it think it is. There is no such thing as 'the thing in itself', a phrase so beloved by Kant.

Vico thought that a correct philosophical conception would enable the historian to solve historical problems. This would enable him to compare the history of remote periods with the present. Vico considered that history moved in cycles, and that between them one could argue that two different periods might have the same general character. He compares the Homeric period of Greek history and the European Middle Ages – these are heroic periods which have a warrior aristocracy, an agricultural economy, and respect for personal prowess. A study of the Middle Ages would enable us to learn more about the Homeric age than Homer can tell us. It seems strange that this should be so, but on reflection we can see that there is much truth in the idea.

It is not sufficient for a modern historian to study a particular past period. The examination of authentic documents and archaeological artefacts is insufficient; the historian must do everything possible to steep himself in the past.

If he is studying England at the time of the Norman Conquest, his historical knowledge would tell him that England was not really a nation. It was still basically the Heptarchy – the land of the Seven Kingdoms; a nation very rarely loses its independence because of one defeat.

In the Franco-Prussian war of 1870, France suffered two crushing defeats at Metz and Sedan but this did not mean that France had lost her independence. Even in the Second World War, when France was occupied by the Germans, this occupation was only temporary. Against this one could argue that the Germans could have occupied Czechoslovakia and retained it, especially as Britain and France did not object and the Russians would not go to war for the sake of the Czechs, and also because Poland would never allow Russian troops to enter their territory.

Our historian would have to imagine he was a Saxon peasant wearing a collar round his neck to denote his servitude. He would live on 'ombel pie' (humble pie), his life would be 'short, nasty and brutish'; in no way would it be what the Irish call 'craic 90'. 'Craic 90' means 'perfect, marvellous, wonderful'; why *90* is lost in the mists of time. Our expression 'it's not what it's cracked up to be' probably equates 'cracked' with *craic*; the phrase 'the system is cracking up' has the entirely opposite meaning.

Another word which has two opposing meanings is
    cleave = to cut to death
               = to cling to

These verbs with opposite meanings are quite common in languages.

Returning to our historian peasant, he could not improve his lot by fighting the Normans. There were spasmodic attempts at revolt – the struggle by Hereward the Wake springs to mind – but it was a forlorn hope. The Normans rapidly built castles all over the country and introduced the system of feudalism, which established military control of the kingdom by the barons, who swore fealty to the monarch.

Vico further thought that similar periods tended to recur in the same order, after which there is a decline into barbarism. We may make a comparison by considering society as a caravan lumbering up a steep incline; it cannot remain stationary, for it will roll down. The goal which it is endeavouring to reach is not known. The leaders of the caravan know that they must continue in their movement forward to increase their knowledge of science, the arts, technology and industry. They may not know that there is a time bomb ticking away in the caravan. Contradiction is the law of life. Inside the caravan this shows up as wars, civil wars and the increasing power of self-destructive elements, all of which threaten the existence of the caravan.

Wars have been endemic all through the history of society – town against town, city against city, and nation against nation. At all times great empires have been established, have endured for some time, but finally expired. Archaelogical research has uncovered many of the artefacts of ancient times and reconstructed their way of life. This is especially true of the Middle East as a whole and particularly Israel, which is very rich in *tels* (hillocks) and which are yielding rich findings to the archaeologists, whose discoveries in very many instances corroborate the Biblical version.

The very name Armageddon tells us its history. Israel was the middle ground, the cockpit, in which the Egyptian and Assyrian Empires waged their continual warfare. Well before Machiavelli the ancient world accepted that it was the duty of the monarch or ruler to enlarge his empire or kingdom, and nowhere was it better exemplified than in the case of Rome.

Rome began life as an ordinary city. Fable has it that it was founded by Romulus and Remus, who had been suckled by a she-wolf. The qualities of the Roman citizen soon began to manifest themselves. Discipline, steadfastness and respect for law, evoked the admiration of other cities, the inhabitants of which were only too proud to proclaim that they were Romans. Gradually the boundaries of Rome expanded, until the time came that it clashed with Carthage in Northern Africa. The series of Punic Wars began. At first the Carthaginians, led by great generals such as Hamilcar and his son Hannibal, were successful. Hannibal accomplished the incredible feat of crossing the Alps in wintertime. The fortunes of Rome at this time were very low, but the Romans were determined not only to defend themselves but to destroy Carthage: *'Cartago delenda est,'* and under Scipio Africanus they achieved this. The city was sown with salt and was no more.

The last important enemy was never replaced, the path of Rome to greater achievements was unimpeded, further horizons beckoned. The Romans very soon responded. They made their task easier by building magnificent roads throughout their domain. Soon 'all roads led to Rome'. In Britain the roads they built lasted for many centuries – the speed of movement which these roads made possible was a very important factor in aiding them to retain their rule. It is interesting to note that the Romans did not wish to extend their frontiers without limit. They tried to limit their boundaries to Germany but they had already become too extended. In AD7 they suffered an unexpected attack by German tribes and they lost two legions. The Emperor Augustus demanded of Varus, the Roman commander: 'Where are my legions, Varus?'

The British who had learnt this lesson tried to limit their rule in India to the North West Frontier but could not avoid being attacked from time to time by Pathans. Their losses, however, were moderate compared to those suffered by the Romans.

Machiavelli in the fifteenth century was the first statesman to promulgate the theory that it was the duty of the prince to enlarge his state by whatever means possible. He anticipated Von Clausewitz, who in the nineteenth century said that military action could be taken to further political objectives. It is interesting to note that well into the twentieth century International Law accepted the validity of military conquest. When in 1936 Italy invaded Abyssinia and conquered it, the King of Italy was accepted as Emperor and, furthermore, all debts owed to Haile Selassie, the erstwhile ruler, would have to be paid to the King-Emperor. This would not be tolerated nowadays by the United Nations which has replaced the old League of Nations, and does not recognise military conquest.

It is true, however, that the former Soviet Union acquired vast territories as a result of the Second World War, and would not budge from them.

The collapse of the Union has liberated these territories, although the Congress of Independent States (CIS) as it is now called, still retain the Japanese Kurile Islands and, despite their urgent economic need to placate the Japanese, are as yet immovable on this point.

We come now to examine the problems of civil wars, which differ according to the nations involved and the periods in which they took place.

The first civil war we will examine is that in England (1642–1649). This was not a war of classes, as some Marxists might aver, but a war in which brother opposed brother, father and son opposed each other, aristocrat opposed aristocrat and merchant opposed merchant. There were of course various parts of the country which were stronger in their convictions. Soon the parties emerged as Cavaliers and Roundheads. The latter were led by Oliver Cromwell, a Huntingdon squire: 'Old Noll, warts and all.' The Cavaliers were led by Prince Rupert of the Rhine, the King's nephew, but the Roundheads also had military leaders like Lord Manchester on their side. They, the Roundheads, were chagrined at being so described but they could not find an appropriate disparaging soubriquet for their opponents – the Cavaliers had won in the propaganda war. This success did not however help them to secure London to their side. London, even in the seventeenth century, was a mighty city and its support of one side would be decisive; and so it turned out to be. Its support for the Roundheads destroyed the theory of the Divine Right of Kings.

One would have thought that this would have an effect on the neighbouring French monarchy, but it did not. The French King Louis XIV, '*le roi soleil*' (the Sun King), so strongly maintained his position that he was able to say, 'I am the State' (*l'État, c'est moi.*) In spite of the miseries and distress which Louis' lust for conquest caused the French people, they did not revolt, and he lived to the age of 77, without let or hindrance. The storm would break after him: 'After me, the deluge.' And so it proved to be.

The French Revolution of 1789 was a frightful civil war. The Sansculottes (the trouserless ones) seized the Bastille on 14th July, they massacred the guards, and decapitated the governor De Launay, thrusting his head on a pike and parading it through the city. Thousands of aristocrats were massacred by the new execution method, perfected by Dr Guillotine and which bears his name. The tumbrils, bringing the victims to the place of execution, rumbled continuously through the city, whilst the French housewives observed the activities whilst knitting and commenting on the heads that were falling as if they were footballs.

The ferocity of the civil war augmented or lessened according to which party was in power. There were two main parties – the Girondins and the Jacobins. The Girondins were led by Danton, whose famous call: '*L'audace, l'audace, toujours l'audace,*' still resounds two centuries after it was first made. The Jacobins were led by Robespierre and they were well to the left of the political spectrum. Interestingly, both men were lawyers, and whilst it could be said that Danton was a Socialist, Robespierre, 'the sea-green incorruptible' could be described as Communist.

The Revolutionaries were not content with success in France but issued a call to all countries in Europe to overthrow their rulers. Before this evoked a response from these rulers, especially those of Prussia and Austria, there was an attempt by the Vendéans and the Vendée area of France to overcome the Revolution. In response the Jacobins established the Committee of Public Safety. Incidentally, KGB is the exact equivalent Russian style.

To celebrate the Revolution, Rouget de L'isle composed the Battle Hymn of the Republic, the 'Marseillaise' and there can be no doubt that its stirring tones enthused and stimulated the Revolutionaries:

'*Aux armes, citoyens!*'

The Armies of Prussia and Austria now invaded France, and the mettle of the Revolution was tested in 1792 at the Battle of Valmy, at which Goethe, the great German writer, was present. The 'Cannonade of Valmy' was a complete success for the French – a successful invasion of France was now out of the question; what was far more probable was that French arms would be ready to spread the ideas of the Revolution throughout Europe.

'The occasion brings forth the man.' – Napoleon!

In January 1793 the French executed their King Louis XVI and in September of that year they executed their queen, Marie Antoinette: 'If they have no bread, let them eat cake.' Her insensitivity to the people's miseries, which is indicated by her remarks, no doubt was an important factor in deciding her fate.

Yet in 1804, Napoleon, after being the First Consul, was able to become Emperor of the French. Thus in eleven years the French had made a complete *volte-face*; one of the results of this was a prolonged war with the other powers in Europe which ended with the defeat of the 'Little Corporal'. This defeat was only made possible by the resistance of Britain. In the words of William Pitt, Prime Minister of Britain in 1797:

'We have saved ourselves by our exertions, and Europe by our example.'

The next civil war in France took place in 1870. It arose out of the policy of Napoleon III, Emperor of the French. He had been President of France until, by a *coup d'état* in 1852, he became Emperor. He had, however, become increasingly unpopular and thought he would offset this by waging a successful war. This is a stratagem which has often been employed to assuage popular discontent. A later example of this policy was the Russo-Japanese War in 1904, when the Russian Tsar thought that an easy victory, of which he was certain, would abate popular discontent. His defeat served only to inflame it. So it proved with Napoleon. He had no idea that he was playing right into the hands of Bismarck, the Prussian Chancellor, whose policy of 'Blood and Iron' was to wage wars at his own time and selection. He had already waged two successful wars; the first was against Denmark in 1864, whereby he gained Schleswig Holstein; the second was war with Austria whereby if successful he would eliminate Austria's influence in Germany. He was indeed successful.

Austria was defeated at the Battle of Koniggratz (Sadowa) in 1866, but Bismarck's attitude to their defeat was so conciliatory that Austria remained under Prussian influence. This influence was so strong that Austria allied itself to Germany in the first World War, 1914–1918. The Central Powers (Germany and Austria) proved a very hard nut to crack. The result of the war was the emergency of another Corporal, Corporal Schickelgruber, alias Hitler.

Hitler very early on realised that his name would arouse only mirth every time it was mentioned. Is it fanciful to imagine that Schickelgruber could never have seized power in Germany? The importance of a vehicle does not depend entirely on its performances; it must also bear an appropriate name.

In this connection we might remind ourselves of two observations made by Bismarck. The first was: 'The master of Bohemia is the master of Europe.' The master of Bohemia was Austria, but Austria was very far from being the master of Europe.

His other observation, however, was of an entirely different order: 'The most significant feature of the nineteenth century is the fact that England and America speak the same language.' Although he said this after war between England and America had broken out in 1812, he concluded that this was merely an isolated hiccup – it would never occur again. History has confirmed Bismarck's view – England and America have become firm friends and allies, as witness the two World Wars, and the recent war in the Persian Gulf.

Chapter 12

The next civil war we have to deal with took place in France in 1871. A year previously, France had been at war with Prussia and had been defeated. Prussian troops invested Paris and stood by whilst the popular discontent boiled over and expressed itself in the appearance on the political scene of the Communards, forerunners of the Communist Party. The Communards proclaimed the birth of the Commune. They stained their standard by murdering the Archbishop of Paris. Thiers, head of the Government, 'the monstrous Gnome', as Marx called him, exacted a terrible revenge. Thousands were killed in Paris; the Père Lachaise cemetery was filled to overflowing; thousands more were sent to perish miserably on Devil's Island.

There is no doubt that this horrendous treatment led in Paris to the creation of the 'Red Belt', which comprised a number of Parliamentary seats held by the Communist Party for many years. It is only recently that this grip has loosened, and the Communist vote has dropped from 20% to about 10%, roughly equal to that of the Fascist Party, led by Le Pen.

It is strange to think that the destruction of Naziism in Germany has not led to its obliteration elsewhere. In Yugoslavia at the present time it is given a new name: 'ethnic cleansing'. This 'cleansing' is a result of the divergence of ethnicity, although there is a greater ethnic relationship between Serbs and Croats, as they speak almost the same language. The Serbs use both the Cyrillac and the Latin alphabets, whilst the Croats use the Latin one. There is also a difference in religion, the Serbs being Greek Orthodox, whilst the Croats are Catholic. There is of course a large Muslim population in Bosnia. These populations had lived together peaceably for hundreds of years as part of the Austrian Empire.

Many historians had predicted that so long as a Turkish threat to Austria continued there would be peace in Yugoslavia. As soon as the Turkish threat ceased to exist, the Empire would fall asunder and the constituent elements would begin their own independent life. And so it was. It is regrettable that this resurgence was marred by ethnic divergence. Is it possible to initiate a programme of ethnic convergence? Under the present circumstances, no such possibility exists until the combatants have battered themselves into exhaustion, as did the Protestants and Catholics in the 30 Years War.

Chapter 13

We now turn to examine the civil war in the United States during the period 1861–1865, between North and South. The North was highly industrial and had abolished slavery and groups of Northerners had arranged methods to enable black slaves from the South to escape to the North.

Abraham Lincoln, President of the United States, had said, 'A house, which is half free and half slave cannot stand.'

The Southern leader, Jefferson Davis, wished to withdraw from the Union, but Lincoln refused to accept his apparently not unreasonable request. He realised that such a split would be ruinous for both parties – the South *had* to stay in the Union, and *had* to abolish slavery. This could not be done without civil war, but this was conducted in a humane way. Both sides tried to slap pejorative names onto each other, but the best they could employ was the North calling the South 'Johnny Reb' and the South calling the North 'Yanks'.

Although the North was vastly superior in numbers and in industrial capacity, their generals were not very able, whilst the South had a leader of genius in General Robert E Lee. In addition the South had an advantage in that, being farmers and plantation owners, they took more easily than the North to military life. The South were able to continue the war for several years, until General Grant of the North took command and his able deputy General Sherman made his famous march to the sea, 'marching through Georgia'. This put the finishing touch to Southern resistance and in the spring of 1865 they surrendered.

One result of the Civil War has been that the South for over a hundred years has returned Democrats to the American Congress and Senate. Only recently has this process thawed and Republicans have been able to make some progress.

Chapter 14

We now examine the course of civil war in Russia in February and October 1917.

Tsarist Russia had by February 1917 been engaged as ally of Britain and France in the First World War against Germany, Austria and Turkey. By attacking East Prussia in August 1914, the Russians prevented an early victory by the Germans who would otherwise have taken Paris.

The Russians sustained a crushing defeat at Tannenberg. This was the second battle there which history records. At the first battle, in 1410, the Knights of the Teutonic Order were overwhelmingly defeated by the army of Poland, Lithuania under Jagellon. Sienkiewicz, the great Polish writer, describes in moving tones the reactions of Jagellon as he surveyed the battlefield where he had gained so great a victory. This victory alleviated in some degree the misery and tears suffered by the Slavic lands at the hands of the Teutons.

This second battle of Tannenberg ended the Russian threat to East Prussia. The German-Austrian armies were now able to advance in Poland. Russian industry, very backward compared to the Central Powers, could not supply the arms required to enable Russia to continue the war; neither could Russian agriculture supply the food which the population required. Britain and France could not provide food either. As a result, food riots broke out in Russia.

The Cossacks, hitherto the unquestioning Praetorian Guard of the Tsars, were sent out to quell the unrest of the masses, but they displayed sympathy with them. In the meantime soldiers of the front became furious at being sent there without arms and having to wait for comrades to be killed so that they could then use their weapons. They deserted in myriads. By February 1917 the Russian military and industrial machines had broken down completely. The Tsar, who had wanted to leave Tsarskoe near St. Petersburg, found that not only was no transport available, but there were growing and insistent calls for his abdication. The Tsar, Nicholas II, would at first not hear of it, but then decided to try to save the throne by persuading his uncle to take it. This he did not wish to do, and thus Tsarist rule, the Romanoff dynasty, was finally extinguished.

Little did the Romanoffs, who had celebrated their 300 years of occupation of the throne, realise how short this would now be. Gone were the glories of Peter the Great and Catherine the Great, named 'Semiramis of the North' for her sexual activities.

The Romanoffs were destined to die miserably in the town of Yekaterinburg in 1918 at the hands of a local Bolshevist group. Stories later emerged that one of the members of the royal family, Anastasia, had managed to escape, and for some years afterwards the international press was engaged in speculation as to whether or not she was an imposter; but it appears to be more probable that she was.

With the abdication of the Tsar, a provisional government was set up with Prince Llov as leader. In his cabinet there was Alexander Kerensky as Minister of Justice. He soon became Minister of War and in August became leader of the Government.

In the meantime the Bolsheviks (*majority* people) had become very active and with the arrival of their leader Nicholay Lenin began to prepare for a *coup d'état*; they did not expect to succeed, but Lenin said that such an opportunity was unlikely to recur soon and if they lost their lives it would be easier for their successors. The Bolsheviks were prepared to give their lives for the cause; their opponents, the Mensheviks, were not. 'He who dares wins,' is the verdict of history.

The Bolsheviks fully expected their victory to be emulated everywhere and especially in Germany. There was some revolutionary activity there, the leaders of which were Karl Liebknecht and Rosa Luxemburg, but it was not powerful. The leaders of the Social Democratic Party, Ebert and Noske, proved to be reactionary and did their utmost to crush the 'Spartacus movement' as it was called after the Roman slave Spartacus, who unsuccessfully led the revolt against Rome in the year 133 BC.

Chapter 15

Numerous civil wars have been raging in many African countries, which had formerly been colonies of the Great Powers. These wars vary in type according to the different motives of the parties concerned.

In Nigeria civil war erupted because one of its provinces, Biafra, wished to be independent. The revolt was crushed with great brutality. It is ironical that countries which have themselves been colonies adopt an imperialist attitude towards those desiring to attain independence themselves. It is difficult to know how strong the feeling is, simmering amongst the subjugated people. Judging by the general history of the African nations, it is still there and may forcibly express itself at any unexpected moment.

In Angola, formerly a Portuguese colony, civil war had been raging for many years between opposing parties. The Portuguese did not attempt to suppress opposition totheir rule. They quietly moved out and left the field to the native political parties, led by Joseph Savinbi for Unita against the MPLA. Frelimo was led by Samora Machel who died in an aeroplane crash and who was succeeded by Joaquim Chissano, backed by South Africa. Afonos Dhlakama was leader of Renamo. An agreement, arranged by Tiny Rowland and Robert Mugabe, has now (mid-August 1992) been reached by the opponents. Another fire extinguished?

After many years of civil war, the parties managed to come to an agreement, and it is highly probable that it will stick. Here again the combatants have battered themselves to the point of exhaustion.

A similar case is that of Mozambique which had also been a Portuguese colony and which also the Portuguese had quitted.

For more than fifteen years civil war has raged between the two opposing parties, Frelimo and Renamo. More than a million lives have been lost, millions more have lost their homes and have been rendered destitute and subject to famine and disease. Only humanitarian aid on a massive scale can help to avoid a horrendous catastrophe.

In Rhodesia, a former British colony established by Cecil Rhodes after whom it was named, civil war between black and white was averted by the action of the British Government. Ian Smith, leader of the whites in Rhodesia, had declared that 'never in a thousand years would the whites accept black supremacy'. The British Government endeavoured by a policy of sanctions to blockade Rhodesia. This policy did not prove successful as many firms throughout the world found trade with Rhodesia to be very profitable, and the British navy proved to be inadequate for the task.

The Government, however, decided to try negotiation. They called Ian Smith and the black leaders Robert Mugabe and Joshua N'komo to a conference. Mugabe was the leader of the Shona tribe and N'komo the leader of the Matabele tribe. The Shonas were far more numerous than the Matabeles and the latter realised that there was no possibility of resisting the Shonas by military means. There was also the fact that Britain favoured Mugabe as against N'komo. These factors ensured a bloodless victory for Mugabe who remains in power to this day, whilst N'komo has retreated into the shadows. Incidentally Mugabe has revealed his true racist attitude by a recent remark when he spoke of some person that the latter was hard-hearted enough to be a Jew! Did Mugabe, who receives vast aid from the British Government, ever request that the amount provided by the Jewish taxpayer here should be deducted from the sum he receives? One has only to ask the question to realise that the answer from Mugabe is, 'You give and we take.' His complaint is that he does not receive enough – he could never receive enough.

As soon as he came to power Mugabe changed the country's name to Zimbabwe. He realised the importance of erasing old names and establishing new ones; it was important for him to erase old associations and connections as soon as possible.

His example was followed in South West Africa, where the native population had been struggling for years against rule by South Africa. Its political expression was SWAPO (South West Africa Political Organisation) and when SWAPO won the struggle they immediately renamed the country Namibia and it remains so to this very day.

Chapter 16

The most recent manifestation of civil war is that in Yugoslavia, where it is still raging today between Serbs, Croats and Bosnians (August 1992). If we examine the conflict between Serbs and Croats we find it difficult to see why there is one. Both peoples speak practically the same language which is thus called Serbo-Croat. The Serbs use both the Cyrillac and Latin alphabets, whilst the Croats use the Latin one. There is a difference in religion. The Serbs are Greek Orthodox whilst the Croats are Catholics, but this has never been a matter for conflict, such as raged in Germany in the seventeenth century.

The Bosnians are Muslims. The three communities had however lived together in harmony for centuries as part of the Austro-Hungarian Empire until the outbreak of the Second World War in 1939. Germany invaded Yugoslavia and the Croats decided to join them against Serbia. They acquired the name of Chetniks, and they behaved cruelly and ferociously towards the Serbs although they were much milder towards the Bosnians.

'The occasion brings forth the man', an old historical saying, was exemplified by the appearance of Tito, a Croat, who organised and led the resistance to the German occupation. The activities of the partisans, as they were called, tied down hundreds of thousands of German troops, and were instrumental in disrupting the German military machine's timetable for the invasion of Russia. This disruption proved to be an important factor in the eventual Nazi defeat in the war. Tito became President of Yugoslavia and during his lifetime there was no dissension – all the national groups were at peace with each other.

This happy state of affairs came to a halt after Tito died; the old-time friction burst into explosive force. The civil war has already lasted for two years and there is no end in sight. The situation is complicated by the fact that the Serbian Government is communist, determined to seize as much territory as possible and incorporate as much territory, containing a proportion of Serbs, as possible. The wars in the Balkans of 1913 have now returned with Bosnians as the eye in the storm. The ferocity of the war today far exceeds that of 1913. It is an ethnic war basically, a war of tribes and peoples, a classic illustration of how ethnic divergence leads to 'ethnic cleansing', a euphemism which endeavours to hide its true meaning, i.e. the dispossession and dispersion of the losing side. Once this process is started it is like a cancer spreading continuously in all directions; in the case we are now considering, from Moldova to Albania, the Urals to the Adriatic, Armenia and Azerbajan.

Nations which had painfully and laboriously developed from tribes are slipping back; the lumbering caravan of humanity in its steep upward climb on the road to progress and improvement is faltering. Especially so is this the case with Bosnia, where its Moslem population was first recorded as a separate people in the 1971 census, confirmed by Tito's constitution of 1974. The Serbs and Croats now resent this, saying that the Moslems are really Serbs and Croats forcibly converted by the Ottoman Turks.

There could be a considerable amount of truth in this assertion. In 1915 Tallat Pasha, head of the Turkish Government, committed genocide against his Armenian subjects, massacring 1½ million of them. The Turks have consistently denied this, but there is unimpeachable documentary evidence to prove their guilt. Their treatment of the Kurds over many years and extending to the present day is cruel in the extreme. The Kurdish language is not recognised; there are no Kurdish schools. If a Kurd wishes to pursue a legal claim against anybody for whatever reason, the court will not accept his language – only Turkish is recognised; the Kurd must speak Turkish. If he cannot do so he must find someone to do so for him and if he cannot he may not go to court. The Bosnian Moslems, according to the Census of 1991, made up 44% of Bosnia's population and were the fastest growing minority in Yugoslavia.

The international community has tried to establish a security system to deal with a Europe of the peoples and the minorities. The final act of the Helsinki Conference tries to deal with this problem by laying down the guidelines for the Conference on Security and Co-operation in Europe (CSCE): 'The participating states regard as inviolable all one another's frontiers as well as the frontiers of all states in Europe and therefore they will refrain now and in the future from assaulting these frontiers.' The frontiers cannot be altered even where the rights and freedoms of all peoples and minorities are concerned: they should be allowed security and self-determination but no more.

This declaration is rejected by extremists in Croatia and Serbia, and very forcibly by Macedonian Slavs who now want independence. The Greeks do not accept that the Macedonians are a nation, and consider that their action was instigated by a ploy by Tito to seize Thessalonika and reach the Aegean. They have so far stalled EC recognition by the European Commision by casting a veto until Macedonia agrees to change the name of its republic. (The name means fruit salad in French and Italian.)

It also has its minorities, Albanians, Turks and Serbs, and Serbia also has large minorities. There are 380,000 Hungarians in Vojvodina, 1.8 million in Kossovo and thousands of Moslems in the Sanyak of Novi Pazar. If the Albanians in Kossovo were involved, the war would cross Yugoslavia's old frontiers and become truly Balkan – Bulgaria, Turkey and possibly Greece could be sucked in. Albania has a Greek minority of about 300,000 (population 3.2 million). Bulgaria has more than 1 million Moslems. Under the Communist régime of Todor Zhivkov they were being forced to change their name and religion, and hundreds of thousands of them fled to Turkey.

Romania presents an even more complicated ethnic problem, with nearly 2 million Hungarians and about 1.7 million Protestants. The communist leader of Romania had plans to drive the Hungarians out. However, revolt in Romania succeeded in overthrowing him, and thus saving the Hungarians. The latter, however, are uneasy, not knowing what any turn in events in Romania might have in store for them.

Further east in the Dobruja area, stretching across the Danube delta, there is a remarkable array of relics of the *Volkerwanderung* (migration of peoples of ancient times). Here there are Lipovians (Russian old believers), Tatars, Turks and Gagauz (Christian Turks), whilst in the north there is a community of Greeks.

The most explosive ethnic mixture is in what was the Soviet republic of Moldova where many people have suffered violent deaths since the fall of the Ceausescus in 1989. A Russian colony in Moldova had been set up by Stalin to bring industry to the rich area on the River Dniester. This colony has now set up its own republic of Trans-Dniester, although many ethnic Romanians would prefer to be part of Romania itself – of the population of about 700,000 about 60% are Romanian, 20% Ukrainian and 20% Russian.

The Hungarian Government is increasingly worried about the fate of large numbers of its citizens scattered throughout the Balkans, especially in Vojvodina in Serbia, in Transylvania and in Slovakia; in the latter they number about 600,000 out of a population of 5 million.

It is agreeable to note a difference of attitude in other countries. Czechoslovakia, land of Czechs and Slovaks, has seen a pleasant separation between the two peoples – they go their respective ways without rancour or hate.

There are other minorities who calmly straddle state borders. About 800,000 Ruthenian and Slav adherents of the Uniate Church, which combines Catholicism with Greek Orthodoxy, are living peacefully within Trans-Carpathia on the borders of Slovakia and Ukraine.

Other minorities have practically all faded from the Balkans now, and those who do not have a national homeland face an uneasy future. One such is the Vlachs, a Latin-speaking shepherd people of 250,000 living obscurely between northern Greece, Romania and Hungary.

The 1991 Yugoslav census showed that there were 1.33 million Yugoslavs of mixed Serb, Croat or Moslem parentage, now a people without a state.

Holocaust and war have reduced the population of Jews in the Balkans to under 30,000, and there are fewer than 20,000 Armenians.

A barely recognised group are the Gipsies. There are 300,000 in Slovakia alone, 200,000 each in Yugoslavia and Bulgaria, up to 1 million in Hungary, and up to 2 million in Rumania. They are the fastest growing single minority in Europe. With 5 million in the Balkans and Central Europe alone, there are all told now 15 million. They are however treated as social outcasts and play no part whatever in the economic and political life of the countries in which they live. The Gipsies have no desire or interest in taking part in such activities – they are struggling for survival.

We may make a comparison between two different historical processes which we describe as Africanisation and Balkanisation. In the first case, Africans who have been tribesmen for centuries are now endeavouring to reach the status of nationhood. We may note in this case the appropriateness of a comparison with the efforts of the Jews before they reached Israel. The Bible speaks of the twelve tribes of Israel and the apportionment of the land to the tribes, with a special arrangement for the priestly tribe, the Levis. The tribal boundaries have long since disappeared. Continuous movement between them has helped the tribes to reach the status of nationhood. Today nobody refers to 'the tribes of Israel'. They have acquired the status of nationhood. Even the Arab enemies of Israel do not speak of it as tribal. They refer to it as 'the Zionist Entity'.

We find, however, that in Europe today a diametrically opposing force is operating what we have described as 'Balkanisation', where Balkan nations are reverting to tribalism. In some cases this is the signal for the emergence of civil war, as we have seen, for instance, in Yugoslavia. In other cases, such as in Czechoslovakia, this separation has been peacefully accomplished. This is reminiscent of what happened just before the second world war in Czechoslovakia. There the Sudetan Germans had lived in the foothills for centuries, quietly and normally, without being in any way harassed by the Czech government. Their leader Henlein, egged on by Hitler, now began to complain loudly and vociferously that his people were being bitterly oppressed by the Czechs. Goebbels, Hitler's propaganda chief, an evil man, but very capable, took up the case. How could these sub-humans (*Untermenschen*) oppress members of the Aryan race, the master race (*Herrenvolk*)? This is a striking exemplification of the use and manipulation of language for political, and other, purposes.

We can cite a number of other examples: 'Sheeny' for Jew; 'Huns' for Germans; 'Scratch a Russian and you find a Tartar'; 'Nigger lovers'; 'Indian (Redskins) lovers' are expressions which show up the sentiments and feelings of the speakers. We are now in a position to note the meritability of language.

Chapter 17

There has long been an expression in English: 'safe as houses'. To acquire one's own house has long been a dream of ordinary people, and since the middle of the century it has been increasingly realised. Possession meant stability, a solid asset, unassailable. What could be better and safer than to put one's money into bricks and mortar? For many years the price of houses continued to rise.

In 1935 it was possible to buy a three-bedroom house in Hanworth, West London, for £395 – a deposit of £25 secured. A four-bedroom house, semi-detached in Surbiton, could be bought for £800.

People began to see the opportunities for making money by dealing in the property market. Buy and sell, and make an ever-increasing profit.

Not all house buyers were interested in so doing – they were satisfied to have a house of their own – but there were many who used their house as a means of making money. After all, 'what is safer than houses'? With the recession which we are now experiencing, and which shows no signs of improvement, the picture has been radically altered. The position now is that house owners are finding that the mortgage they are holding is greater than the value of the property, and many thousands of house owners – whose numbers are steadily increasing – are being compelled to leave their houses. The building societies are making every effort to stem the flood, but so far (August 1992) this has not been very successful. There is here a Catch 22 situation. The housing market will not improve whilst the recession lasts; the recession will continue until the housing market improves.

In accordance with Vico's cyclical view of the historic process, the Russian economist Kondratyev maintains that there is a forty-year cycle in economic affairs in all lands, advanced or not, but stronger in the First

World than elsewhere. He maintains that this cycle is unavoidable, and that industrial and financial leaders should meet at regular and frequent intervals to address themselves to this problem.

Chapter 18

A striking example of the influence of language on the minds of people is the word 'hands'.

Factories at times will put out notices: 'Hands wanted' or 'No hands wanted'. Sometimes they will advertise in the press: 'Hands wanted' – they will not advertise 'No hands wanted'.

To the employers, hands are the only part which they require of the worker. One could imagine from their attitude that if they could somehow detach the hands they would do so, and return them to the worker's body when required. What is surprising is the attitude of the workers themselves. They have become so brainwashed that they accept this derogatory attitude. Trade unions, when in dispute with employers, do not challenge this concept – certainly not in times of recession. So long as they continue to accept this description of themselves, so long will it continue.

Another interesting phrase which has acquired fresh meaning is 'new age traveller'. 'Traveller' once meant one who travels, either for pleasure or to see new sights in different areas of the world. If he did so for business purposes, he would be a commercial traveller. The new age traveller does none of these things; he is not engaged in any kind of work – he is a 'Hippy'. If he travels anywhere at all it is to 'a rave' which has also acquired an additional contrary meaning. We can say

1. He raves   He is insane, speaks nonsense
2. He raves   He is frantic with delight

We also have the noun 'rave'. He or she is going to a 'rave' where they will have what they consider to be a wonderful time.

Similarly the word 'burn up' meaning:
1. conflagration
2. a good time, similar to rave

3. to use up, e.g. 'He burned up his energy in trying to solve the problem.'

Another example of that bane of language, verbs with opposite meanings, is 'chuff'. We can say:
1. He is chuffed   He is happy, delighted
2. He is chuffed   He is upset, chagrined

Another example is 'browned off'.
1. The roast is nicely browned off.
2. He is browned off, meaning he is upset or fed up.

The latter term might smack of colloquialism but it is sometimes difficult to draw a precise border line.

We can cite some examples from other languages. In Spanish, '*Olé*' expresses delight and satisfaction. The roar of enthusiasm in which the Spaniard expresses his excitement at a bull fight is an indirect contrast for *mañana* (tomorrow) meaning; do not do today what you can do tomorrow. As tomorrow never comes, nothing is ever done and this is one sound reason for the decline of Spain from being the leading European power in the sixteenth century, when it drew from its colonies in South America huge amounts of treasure. The 'treasure ships', as they were called, were subject to attacks by English freebooters like Sir Francis Drake.

The Spanish navy was also backward in its equipment and naval strategy. The Armada failed in its attempt to make the English Channel negotiable to the Spanish army under Alva in the Low Countries. It had powerful guns, in comparison with which Drake's guns were puny, but the manoeuvrability of the English fleet more than compensated for this. The Armada was decisively defeated, and Spain all but faded as a naval power. It had only been successful against the Turkish fleet at the battle of Lepanto in 1571, but the Turks had never been a strong naval power.

Even in conjunction with the French fleet during the Napoleonic wars, they suffered a decisive defeat at Trafalgar at the hands of the English fleet under Nelson. 'England expects that every man will do his duty,' and they did. One result of the battle was that French naval officers wear a black circle on their jacket sleeves to this day.

Chapter 19

There are some interesting examples of words of *double entendre* which we can take, for example:
1. 'I'll be damned if I will do as you say.'
2. 'I'm blessed if I will do as you say.'

The first expression may be a little more emphatic than the second, but the general sense is very similar.

There are many cases where the meaning of the words employed can only be ascertained if we consider the whole sentence in which these words are found. For example: 'The boy pulled the wool over his friend's eyes.' We could extract no meaning from this sentence if we took each word one by one; we must take the whole sentence and this type of sentence we call exothermic. On the other hand if we say: 'The boy lives in a three-bedroom house with a garden and garage', we can take the words separately and it would make perfectly good sense. Such a sentence we could describe as endothermic.

Interesting examples abound of how particular phrases have special meanings, for example: 'the life of Riley'. If we say of someone that 'he leads the life of Riley', we do not mean that his life is similar to that of an Irishman called Riley. We mean that he leads a wonderful, splendid and most pleasant life – the nearest approach to this is the Italian '*la dolce vita*' and we consider it appropriate to equate the two.

There is a famous Italian phrase: '*Eppur si muove*', which we have incorporated into our own language. It means 'Yet it moves'. The historical background relates to Galileo, the famous astronomer of the sixteenth and seventeenth centuries. Galileo accepted the theory of the heliocentricity of the earth: that is, that the earth revolved around the sun. This theory opposed Catholic dogma, which maintained the exact opposite. Galileo was hauled before the Inquisition who were ready to submit him to the torture if he did not relinquish his views. He was not strong enough however to be tortured, and who could blame him for this? The Inquisition was notorious for its grisly devices of torture. Galileo recanted, but as he did so, he muttered: *'Eppur si muove,'* 'and yet it [the earth] still moves', and this phrase has achieved fame now for nearly four hundred years. If two Italians are engaged in a discussion of any kind, and one is not convinced by the reasoning of the other but cannot convincingly refute it, he will say, *'Eppur si muove.'*

This may be compared with the pre-eminence of English in the world of sport. Cricket, football, rugby, boxing, have been accepted by other languages, as these cannot find an appropriate renaming. This is specially true of Russian which also adds 'businessmen', 'boy scout' and 'boxing' to its borrowings.

An interesting example of masculine arrogance is shown in the Russian language by its reference to 'prodigal son' as *'bloodnye'* (blood like hood); but 'prodigal daughter', if one could imagine such a thing, would be *'bloodnitsa'*, a fornicatress.

Although in general superior cultures manage to impose themselves upon inferior ones, there are exceptions. For instance, in the United States, the Algonquin Indian word for child, papoose, has become acceptable in American English. It is interesting to note that the Redskins (Red Indians) never attained the status of nationhood. For centuries before the coming of the white man the tribes warred against each other. There were various combinations of tribes at different times, but at no time did they ever think of uniting. One important reason for this was their migratory way of life. The enormous expanse of the United States was only able to support a million or two Indians. The latter were indifferent towards the natural resources of the land, indeed they were hardly aware of their existence. Early in the seventeenth century they encountered the white man in the area of what became known as New York, so named in honour of the English Duke of York; they exchanged the land for a handful of trinkets and gee-gaws.

Later, they became embroiled in the seven years war (1756–1763) between England and France. Macaulay, the brilliant English historian and narrator, has described in vivid prose the course of this struggle, where both countries sought the support of the Indians. In the decisive battle of the Heights of Abraham in Canada, the English were victorious although their commander General Wolfe was killed, as was also the French commander, General Montcalm. Wolfe was an unusual soldier; he had said that if he could have written Gray's 'Elegy in a Country Churchyard' (Stoke Poges) he would have preferred that to any number of military victories.

The victory did not mean that Canada would remain British. The French population in Canada continued to grow at a much faster rate than that of the British. Both languages, English and French, continue to be used in Canada, but French is beginning to outdistance English, especially so in Quebec. Here a couple of decades ago the French President, General de Gaulle, made what can only be described as an inflammatory speech, inciting the Québecois: '*Vive le Québec libre!*' Quebec has been bilingual for many years, but French has been steadily outdistancing English, and if matters continue on their present course, it will be only a question of time before English is relegated to a secondary position.

There is however one factor which may help to retard or even halt this movement, and this is American English. This is the tongue of the most powerful nation in the world, and the strength of its language has been demonstrated in the rise of Pidgin English in Africa and especially in Asia. Pidgin is a language of limited vocabulary, according to Collins English Dictionary. It facilitates relationships between people with no common language, and draws its vocabulary almost entirely from a single language.

There are two types of Pidgin: the first is a restricted Pidgin, a minimal contact language that dies when contact is no longer maintained. The second is a developed Pidgin and remains when contact ceases. It becomes a lingua franca between indigenous peoples with no mutually intelligible language. The latter type may eventually become the mother tongue of the community and so acquire the status 'Creole'. Creole may also arise when communities with mutually intelligible languages were kept apart, as was the case with African negroes in America who were separated, as a safety measure, by the white population. Then the community resorts to a Pidgin as the only viable lingua franca, and this then becomes a Creole.

All Pidgins and Creoles examined to date share certain features. They are syntactically simpler than the languages upon which they are based; inflections are minimal and distinctions are made by varying the word order; reduplication is common, as in Jamaica Creole – 'small-small'; Neo-Melanesian – 'talk-talk', and in serial verb structure yielding sentences for instance in Cameroon Pidgin like: 'Dat chief he woman go start begin teach her.'

Creoles and Pidgins based on English exists all over the world and can be divided into two main groups. Atlantic varieties show West African features, and Pacific ones relate to the English used, especially in the late nineteenth and early twentieth centuries, or the China Coast. Most of the vocabulary is based on English but it also includes quite a fair amount of Portuguese; some of these words have percolated into English and have become accepted. Several such words are 'savvy' and 'piccaninny'.

Although in general Creole is inferior to the language of the indigenous people, there are occasions when it sprouts into the grammatically superior tongue, but expresses some sentiments in a sharper and bolder manner and makes a stronger impact. For instance:
1. Long time no see
2. No can do

For the first, we would ordinarily say, 'It's a long time since we saw each other, isn't it?' and for the second, 'I cannot do it.' We can see the difference in impact immediately.

It is said that brevity is the soul of wit, and certainly a long-worded witticism loses its savour precisely because it is long-winded. The moral is – make it short and sharp!

Chapter 20

A striking example of political convergence in Britain is shown by the word 'Butskellism'. This 'ism' is that of R.D. Butler, a power in the Tory Party in the early '60s of this century, and Hugh Gaitskell, leader of the Labour Party. There was also in existence at this time the Liberal Party, but it had been steadily declining in influence, and the other two political parties could afford to ignore it.

The convergence of the parties was so great that they could prepare a social, economic and political policy which satisifed them both. This satisfaction did not last very long. Right wing elements in the Tory Party began to murmur against what they considered to be a sop to socialism, whilst left wing Labourites murmured against their leaders for not proceeding with the class war against the capitalist system.

The leader of the Labour Party at this time was Clement Attlee who was a member of the middle class, and had unexpectedly obtained the position owing to the struggle for leadership between George Lansbury and Ernest Bevin, both of whom belonged to the working class. Lansbury was a Christian Socialist and said, 'He who is not against me is for me,' reversing the old formula of: 'He who is not for me is against me.' An outstanding member of the Labour Party at this time was Nye Bevan, a proletarian if ever there was one, who soon incurred the enmity of Ernest Bevin. Nye Bevan had never received any higher education, but he educated himself and became a brilliant orator whom the Tories feared. When Bevan became an MP he coined the remark: 'The Tories are lower than vermin.' This appellation has struck a chord in left wing Labour circles and is not likely to go out of circulation in the foreseeable future, although it was made some thirty years ago.

In the meantime, significant changes had taken place in the Tory Party. For many years the Marquis of Salisbury had been its Grand Panjundrum and he had strong support from industrial magnates and the landed aristocracy. There was no question here of small business men or members of the working class obtaining a footing in the leadership. But slowly the Tory Party began to converge towards the Labour Party in its selection of leaders. After the retirement of Sir Anthony Eden, Edward Heath, son of a small scale builder, became leader and duly Prime Minister at a Tory victory at the polls in the 1970s. The rise of Edward Heath, now Sir Edward Heath, KG, might not have been enough to make the Marquis of Salisbury turn in his grave, but the election of a woman, the daughter of a grocer, owner of a single small shop, would have been for him the equivalent of the *coup de grace*. (It is interesting, incidentally, how this French word has become part of the English language because it is superior to any possible equivalent.) Had her father been the owner of a supermarket or a number of them, he might have been mollified, but no – only one small shop.

It had long been supposed that Labour, being more progressive and radical, would be the first to provide a woman Prime Minister.

But not only has it not done this, there is in the forseeable future only the prospect of a male Prime Minister. There are some prospective women Cabinet Ministers in the Labour Party, but that is as far as one can go.

The prospect of Labour winning the next election is bleak –they have already lost four in a row, and this has forced Neil Kinnock to resign – he would have been forced to resign at the Labour Party Conference in the autumn, anyway. Many members blame John Smith and his tax proposals for their defeat and they are uneasy at going into battle under his aegis.

The Tories managed to win the General Election in May 1992 despite the continuing recession. Unemployment has been rising steadily, house prices have slumped and businesses of all types are going bust. Even the CBI (Confederation of British Industry), generally a strong supporter of Tory Governments, is highly critical of this one, led by John Major. That a man like John Major could ever become a Tory Prime Minister is a most extraordinary phenomenon. Labour Prime Ministers have generally sprung from the middle class. Atlee was followed by Harold Wilson, an Oxford don. Only James Callaghan could be described as being of working class origin – he had been a seaman. (Incidentally, all three are now Lords – could this be described as a convergence to Tory ideas? It would seem so, even if left wing Labour is in favour of abolishing the House of Lords.) But John Major came of working class stock – he had only gone to an elementary school, he had never been inside a polytechnic or college, and at the age of 16 had been unemployed.

He could be described as a soft leader. Margaret Thatcher was severe with her ministers. If she thought they were not performing well, she was ruthless with them – they had to go, willy-nilly. Amongst those dismissed were Sir Ian Gilmour, Lord St. John Stevas and Sir Leon Brittan. In her behaviour 'the Iron Lady', as she was now called, showed how right this appellation was. She was dynamic, she seemed everywhere at the same time, pressing her views with unabated vigour. She strengthened the ties between Britain and the United States, became the darling of the American public. In twelve years of office she changed Britain and British political behaviour, and has left an indelible stamp upon the face of the land.

John Major lacks this sternness; he cannot bring himself to dismiss a Minister. One such Minister, David Mellor, had been guilty of such behaviour that he proffered his resignation.

Under the circumstances this was the right thing to do, and John Major should have jumped at the opportunity of getting out of embarrassment. He refused to accept the proffered resignation: 'I stick by my friends.' He would not dream of dismissing Norman Lamont, whose performance as Chancellor of the Exchequer has been very lacklustre. He has been maintaining for more than a year now that recovery is just around the corner but that corner has not been turned yet, nor is it likely to be for a long while. Many economists are very gloomy and talk of no possible improvement before 1994, saying that until then the recession will continue to grow.

A Prime Minister cannot fulfil his role if he is soft.

Chapter 21

Continuing our examination of the process of incorporation of words into and from English we find some items of interest in Japanese. Despite the remoteness of Japan from us, and the difficult nature of the language, **kamikaze** and **hara-kiri** have become standard English. In the Second World War Japanese pilots hurled their aircraft with their bombs into enemy targets, although they knew that they themselves must perish. This was 'kamikaze', and we now use this expression when a person commits a desperate and dangerous action: 'He is committing kamikaze'. Curiously, in Japanese the word means 'divine wind'. Hara-kiri (belly cut) describes a ritual suicide by disembowelling with a sword when disgraced or under sentence of death. In England a 'gentleman' who has sinned against the canons of his class, might be 'requested' to do the right thing and blow his brains out; at least this is far less gruesome than hara-kiri.

Suttee describes the former Hindu custom whereby a widow burns herself to death on her husband's funeral pyre. The word derives from Sanskrit – 'Sati' is a virtuous woman. How dazzlingly does this illustrate the sexist nature of this society; a woman can only live if her husband does. 'Male *über alles*', with apologies to the German anthem.

Safari is a word which has the distinction of being Swahili and Arabic; it means an overland journey or hunting expedition especially in Africa. A safari park is a park where wild animals are free to roam and can be observed by people from their cars.

Sahib in India is a word used as a mark of respect to the person thus addressed. This person could use the word after his name, e.g. J Patel

Sahib, much as in Britain we could for example write to John Brown BA or B.Sc or using any other academic distinction he had obtained.

Eminence grise (Grey Eminence) is a French phrase now incorporated into Standard English. It signifies a person who has great influence in high places, although in an unofficial capacity. It originally applied to Father Joseph (François le Clerc du Tromblay) who was father confessor to Cardinal Richelieu in the seventeenth century. Although Richelieu was a prince of the Catholic Church his foreign policy was not determined by his religion. At this time France and Austria were at loggerheads. Although Austria was a Catholic country, Richelieu had dealings with the Turkish Empire which had been steadily increasing its sway in Europe and advancing towards Vienna. They did actually get as far as Vienna in 1683, where they were decisively beaten by John Sobieski, King of Poland. Richelieu bitterly persecuted the French Protestants (Huguenots) in his lifetime – he died in 1642 – but his policy of persecution led to the revoking of the Edict of Nantes by Louis XIV. The edict had been promulgated by Henry IV in 1596 and revoked in 1685. This led to a massive flight of Huguenots from France. Large numbers came to England, especially to the East End of London in Spitalfields where they were able to use their skills in weaving textiles, to the benefit also of the English.

In limbo originally signified the abode of infants who died before they could be baptised and of the just people who died before the advent of Christ; in mediaeval Latin it meant on the border of hell. Nowadays it signifies a place (imaginary) for lost, forgotten or unwanted persons or things. It could also mean an intermediate place or condition between two extremes, or being confined in a prison. Somehow this word has crossed over to the Caribbean, and means a dance, in which dancers pass, while leaning backwards, under a bar.

Assassin originally meant someone who ate hashish, the Arabic word for dried hemp which has the power to induce hallucinations to the eater. In Syria and Persia from about 1100–1250, hashish eaters formed a fanatical secret Muslim sect, which assassinated people with whom they disagreed either from a political or religious point of view; they were particularly eager to kill Crusaders who still remained in Arab lands.

Caliph or '**khalif**' was the title of successors of Mohammed as rulers of the Islamic world assumed by the Sultans of Turkey; the word actually means 'successor' in Arabic. 'Sultan' itself is an Arabic word meaning 'ruler'.

Thug which now describes a violent man or a criminal, derives from Hindi where it means 'thief'. In India, they were a group of robbers and assassins who strangled their victims. Our usage of this word is much more condemnatory than the Hindi one.

Dacoit In India and Burma a dacoit was a member of a gang of armed robbers. In Hindi it means just this.

Shiksa A Jewish name for a non-Jewish girl, and a Jewish one who failed to live up to traditional standards. The male equivalent would be a **sheygets**.

Chazan A man who leads synagogue services as a professional cantor. There are as yet no women chazanim (plural of chazan).

Torah is the Hebrew word which contains the whole body of traditional Jewish teaching, including the Oral Law. It is the scroll on which the Pentateuch is written, used in synagogue services. The word comes from **yara** meaning to instruct.

Kishke A Jewish dish, a beef or fowl intestine or skin stuffed with flour and onions and boiled or roasted. It is also very much favoured by Russians and it could be considered as Russian –they use the same word.

Kreplach A small filled dough casing served in soup.

Lokshen A similar soup based on wheat.

Kvass A Russian drink of low alcoholic strength made from cereals and stale bread. It is also popular in Eastern Europe.

Vodka Also a Russian alcoholic drink, made from grain and potatoes chiefly, but with rectified spirit and water.

Chlop is a Polish word meaning 'peasant', and it has been assimilated into Yiddish with a derogatory meaning. A *Chlop* is a boor, an ignorant and illiterate person. From an onomatopoeic point of view it seems ripe for incorporation into English. **Onomatopoeia** is the forming of words whose sound is imitative of the sound of the noise or action designated, such as 'hiss', 'buzz', 'bang' or 'cuckoo'. Such words are used for poetic or rhetorical effect.

An unusual word is **Witan** or **Witanagemot**, which was an assembly of higher ecclesiastic and important laymen in Ango-Saxon England that met to counsel the king on important matters. *Witan* means 'wise'; 'wit', derived from *Witan*, indicates this when we say, for instance: 'He is a man of wit', or 'he is witty'. We also use the expression 'to wit' which introduces statesments in legal documents.

Kaput A German word expressing complete breakdown and ruin: 'It's all over'; 'We've had it', are the nearest English equivalent phrases. The Germans have another expression for 'We've had it'; *'Es ist mit uns vorbei'*, but this lacks the force of *kaput*. The nearest Jewish equivalent is *'in drerd'*; *drerd* actually means 'floor'; we say in English for example; 'He's on the floor,' which means he is in a bad way, but *in drerd* is much more emphatic.

Shiur A lesson, especially one in which a passage of the Talmud is studied together by a group of people; it actually means 'measurement'.

Talmud is the primary source of Jewish religious laws consisting of the Mishna and Gemara. There are two variations of the Talmud: the Palestinian Talmud of about 375 in the Christian era, or the longer and more important Babylonian Talmud of about the year 500. The word means 'instruction', and a Talmudist is one who specialises in studying it, or who makes a contribution to it.

Mishna is a compilation of precepts passed down as an oral tradition and collected by Judah Ha Nasi (the Prince) in the latter part of the second century. It forms the earlier part of the Talmud; it means 'instruction by repetition'.

Gemara is the main body of the Talmud, consisting of a record of ancient rabbinical debates about the interpretation of the Mishna, and is the primary source of Jewish religious law. It means 'completion'.

Tallith is a white prayer shawl with fringed corners worn over the head and shoulders by men during religious services. A small addition, worn by men under their outer garments, is called **tsitzit**. In Jewish Liberal circles, women wear the tallith and some women are actually Rabbis. This of course is not the case with Orthodox Jewry.

Phylacteries or **tefillim** consist of a pair of blackened square cases containing parchments inscribed with Biblical passages, bound by leather thongs to the head and left arm, which are worn by Jewish men during weekday morning prayers.

Shivah is a period of mourning lasting for seven days from the funeral, during which the mourners do not sit on ordinary chairs, but on low stools. **Shivah** is actually seven (days).

Sanhedrin The supreme judicial, ecclesiastical, and administrative council of Jews in Biblical times, consisting of 71 members. There was also a similar tribunal of 21 members, having less important functions and authority. The word actually means 'seat'.

Samaritan A native of Samaria and is actually short for Good Samaritan. One particular one was noted in Biblical times for helping people in distress or despair. People who commit good deeds are likely to receive this accolade.

Chapter 22

Nirvana In the religion of Buddhism, this secures the final release of mankind from the circle of reincarnation by the extinction of all desires and individual existence, culminating in Buddhism in absolute bliss or in Hinduism in *brahman*.

A **Brahmin** is a member of the priestly class in the rigid Hindu caste system. A **Brahmani** is a woman of this class. So rigid is this system that a Brahmin would feel himself defiled if even the shadow of a member of the lowest class loomed upon him.

How different is this from the life of the Amazons. They were a race of women warriors living in Scythia, near the Black Sea. There are also tales that there were Amazons living in South America. There is actually the River Amazon which flows east through North Brazil to the Atlantic and which is the largest river in the world. This fact would seem to give some credence to this account. Nowadays, if we wish to indicate that a woman is strong and resolute, and aggressive, we would call her an Amazon. An outstanding example of this type of woman is Margaret Thatcher.

Yoga A Hindu system of philosophy aiming at the mystical union of the self with the supreme being in a state of complete consciousness and tranquillity, through various physical and mental exercises. Standing on one's head is one of the exercises which the practitioners consider to be very beneficial. As the number of devotees is continually growing in the West, we can only assume that the system has much merit.

Karma The principle of retributive justice determining a person's state of life, and the state of his reincarnation as the effect of his past deeds and theosophy linked with it, is the doctrine of inevitable consequence for his destiny or fate. **Kismet** is an Arabic word with a somewhat similar meaning to *Karma*. To the Arabs *Kismet* signifies acceptance of the concept that their fate is in the hands of Allah.

Chapter 23

The concept of convergence would never have appealed to Rudyard Kipling (1865–1936), the leading writer and short story writer, who won the Nobel prize for literature in 1907. 'East is East and West is West and never the twain shall meet.' Kipling never stated that the East was inferior to the West, but one can readily infer that this was really his concept.

This is not confirmed by the attitude of white New Zealanders towards the Maoris. The Maoris had lived in New Zealand and the Cook Islands since before the arrival of European settlers. They are descended from Polynesian voyagers who migrated in successive waves from the sixteenth century onwards. Their language is Malay-Polynesian. Their relationship with the white settlers has been good and this was shown in the second World War when the New Zealand Expeditionary Force contained a Maori Battalion. In sporting events, when the New Zealand team play against foreign teams, they always contain some Maoris. The British press has often reported matches between British and New Zealand teams as being matches between Britons and Maoris, just as they would describe matches between 'Brits and Frenchies'.

There have been occasions when there has been irritation and ill-feeling between nations, and this has shown itself in applying insulting language. Thus Britons would call foreigners, and especially Latin and coloured people, Wogs and Wops. The word 'golliwog' is an example of this, as it is a soft doll with a black face, usually made of cloth or rags. Foreigners so far have not come up with similar derogatory epithets. The best appears to be the equivalent of 'perfidious Albion'.

Billabong A stagnant pool in the bed of an intermittent stream or a branch of a river running to a dead end; the word is of native Australian origin and it meant 'long dead'.

Ombudsman A commissioner who acts as an independent referee between individual citizens and the government, central or local. In Britain he is an official without power of sanction or mechanism of appeal, who investigates complaints of citizens against the administration. He is sometimes called Commissioner of Local Administration or Health Service Commissioner or Parliamentary Commissioner. The word is of Swedish origin – the Swedes were the first to establish this system.

Billingsgate is the largest fish market in London; it has been latterly removed to a new site on the Isle of Dogs. In its heyday, it was notorious for the abusive and obscene language used by the workers there. 'To speak Billingsgate' meant that one had reached the nadir of language. The expression 'go to the dogs' meant that one was on the road to ruin, financial or otherwise; it also has the prosaic meaning of going to a dog-racing track.

The violent nature of some breeds of dogs, such as Doberman and Rottweiler, is probably the origin of the phrase '**let loose the dogs of war**'. Such dogs are very useful as guards of property and protection of citizens against violent intruders or robbers.

Nadir The point on the celestial sphere directly below an observer and directly opposite the zenith; it indicates the lowest or deepest point – the nadir of despair. It is not possible to sink lower.

The **zenith** is the exact opposite. When we say of a person that he has reached the zenith of his career, we mean he has reached the top and cannot go any higher.

Daven Originally the Jewish word for prayer. It may be coupled with **mezuzah,** which is a piece of parchment inscribed with Biblical passages and fixed to the doorpost of the rooms of a Jewish house.

It is interesting to note the activities of Christian Missionaries in the early part of the century, especially in the East End of London. There had been a mass immigration of Russian and Polish Jews following the pogrom in 1901. They were poverty stricken and they accepted free medical treatment at the missionary establishment. The missionaries' hopes of a high conversion rate were however not realised. The overwhelming majority of Jews accepted the treatment and ignored the sermons. Despite their poverty they remained true to their faith.

Since the early part of the century, the missionaries have altered their tactics. The Jews in the meantime had enormously improved their position, acquired professional status, and moved to pleasanter districts in North and North West London, and could be fairly described as middle class. Only a very small percentage of Jews remained in the East End, mainly elderly or disabled people without any family.

The missionaries now changed their tactics to cope with the new situation. They now described themselves as Jews for Jesus. They proclaimed that Jesus was a Jew, and they aped traditional Jewish religious customs. They lit candles on the eve of Shabbat (Friday evening), wore *tallitim* (prayer shawls), and adapted various religious practices. They have had considerable success with Jewish students who are living away from home and, apart from several cities such as Manchester and Leeds where there are considerable numbers of Jewish students and a fair number of Jews, are isolated. Some of these students who have not had a religious education at all, or only a superficial one, are falling prey to the blandishments of the missionaries. The Board of Deputies, the supreme Jewish body, is organising a vigorous counter-offensive under the able directorship of Rabbi Arkush, which is yielding some results.

Chapter 24

Casanova Giovanni Jacopo (1725–1798) was an Italian adventurer noted for his Memoirs which give an account of his special life and of contemporary society. His sexual life was so extraordinary that even with the lapse of two centuries, the name of Càsanova is synonymous with large-scale sexuality. 'He's a Casanova' is a phrase to show that the man to whom this applies is sexually very active. 'He's no Casanova' implies the direct opposite.

We may compare this with the expression **Oedipus Complex**. According to Greek myth, Oedipus was the son of Lapus and Jocasta, King and Queen of Thebes. Accidentally he killed his father and unwittingly married his mother, by whom he had four children. When he discovered this he blinded himself, and Jocasta committed suicide. Psychologists use the expression Oedipus Complex in connection with a group of emotions, usually unconscious, of a child, especially a male child, to possess sexually his mother while excluding his father.

This is related to what is called the **Electra Complex**. In Greek mythology Electra was the daughter of Agamemnon, king of Mycenae, who led the Greeks at the siege of Troy. On his return home, he was murdered by his wife Clytemnaestra and her lover Aegisthus. Electra persuaded her brother Orestes to kill their mother and her lover. Psychologists use the expression Electra Complex to explain the sexual attachment of a female child to her father.

Agamemnon had a brother Menelaus; he was a king of Sparta, and the husband of Helen, whose abduction by Paris of Troy led to the Trojan war. 'Was this the face [Helen] that launch'd a thousand ships, and burnt the topless towers of Ilium? [Troy]' has immortalised this event and led to an interpretation of the word 'Trojan'. The Trojans fought with unparalleled tenacity, but the Greeks finally adopted a ruse to give them victory. They constructed a huge wooden hollow figure of a horse which they left outside the city and feigned a retreat; men were concealed inside the figure. The figure was dragged into the city by the Trojans; foolishly they did not examine it. The men concealed inside it opened the city to the final Greek assault.

The ruse was successful; after ten years of war Troy was finally defeated, and it was sacked. The saying now means laying a trap to undermine an enemy. 'To work like a Trojan' means to work long, patiently, and tenaciously, despite the fact that the Trojans lost their war.

Chapter 25

We may pause here for a moment to consider several words with a double and contradictory meaning.
   To **shiver**; it has both a passive and an active meaning:
   a.   to feel very cold, physically or emotionally, e.g. 'he shivered with cold'; he shivered at the very thought.
   b.   to break or smash, as in the words of the Internationale battle hymn of the Communist Parties throughout the world: 'Our own right hand must shiver chains of hatred, greed and fear.'

Objective as in:
   a.   He is objective in his appraisal of the current political situation.
   b.   His objective is to obtain political power in the present situation at all costs.

A word which could be completely opposite to this is 'cliché'.
Cliché is a word or expression which has lost much of its force through over-use; e.g. 'It's got to get worse before it gets better', or an action that has become trite.

Soubriquet or **soubrique** is a humorous epiphet or assumed name or nickname.

Nickname is a familiar pet-name or derisory name given to a person, animal or place. A very tall and powerful man could be described by the use of the word 'tiny'. This has been applied to a prominent figure in our society, Tiny Rowlands, who is the very antithesis of tiny.

Medicine Man Among certain people, especially North American Indians, he is a person believed to have supernatural powers of healing; a magician or sorcerer. If we referred to a doctor as a medicine man it would be a disparaging and belittling remark.

Pharaoh The title of the ancient kings of Egypt. In Egyptian it means a member of a great house.

Pharisee A member of an ancient sect that was opposed to the Sadducees teaching strict observance of Jewish tradition as interpreted by the rabbis, and believing in life after death and in the coming of the Messiah. The name has now degenerated into meaning a self-righteous or hypocritical person. The **Sadducees** were entirely opposed to the Pharisees.

The **Parsees** are adherents of a monotheistic religion of Zoroastrian origin, and were driven out of Persia in the eighth century by the Moslems. This religion now obtains chiefly in Western India.

Zoroastrianism is a dualistic religion founded by Zoroaster, the Persian prophet, in the late seventh or early sixth century BC and is set out in the sacred writings of the Zend-Avesta. Its basic theme is that there is a continuous struggle between Ormazd, the god of light and goodness and his arch-enemy Ahriman, the spirit of evil and darkness; it also includes a highly developed ethical code.

In a lighter vein, we can consider **Shmatte**, originally a Polish word meaning rag. Today it is applied to the tailoring trade: 'We are in the *shmatte* trade' expresses this.

Schlep means to drag something with difficulty. **Schlepper**, which derives from it, has two meanings. The first means somebody employed by a shopkeeper to stand outside the shop and inveigle passers-by to enter it. It is also used in a derogatory sense: 'He is a *schlepper*' indicates one who is not very capable and of whom a capable performance cannot be expected.

Schlemiel is a similar type of word. It means one who could easily be tricked and deceived and would be clumsy and inefficient in whatever he undertook.

Shlemozel originally meant somebody who was unlucky, but the meaning has now changed to describe someone who is clumsy and incompetent.

Some words now of Russian origin:

Samovar A metal urn for making tea, in which the water is heated by charcoal held in an inner container, or nowadays more usually by electricity. In Russian it means 'self-boiling'.

During the French Revolutionary period 1748–1836), and before Napoleon had had himself crowned as Emperor, France was governed by Consuls. The first Consul was Napoleon, the second Barras and the third the Abbé de Sieyes. When Sieyes was asked what he had done during the French Revolution (he had become prominent for his publication of his pamphlet *Qu'est-ce que le troisième état?* (What is the third estate?)) and had helped Napoleon to come to power, he replied '*J'ai survecu*' (I have survived). In this he differed from the Russian Mikoyan. In all the jostling for power amongst the leading members of the Political Bureau, he said he would serve the leader himself but did not wish to be leader.

Troika A Russian vehicle drawn by three horses harnessed abreast; it is also used to indicate a **triumvirate**, akin in meaning to the Spanish **junta** which is a group of military officers holding power, especially after a *coup d'état*. In some parts of Latin America they could be a legislative or executive council.

Junker A member of a group of aristocratic landowners who were devoted to maintaining their identity of extensive social and political privileges. They became the core of the German Army's officer class and were notorious for their arrogant, narrow-minded tyrannical behaviour. In German the word actually means 'young master'.

Hun During the first World War, the Germans were described by the Allies in a very derogatory manner as 'Huns'. Huns were originally members of any of several Asiatic peoples speaking Mongoloid or Turkish languages, who dominated much of Asia and Eastern Europe from before 300 BC. They invaded the Roman Empire in the fourth and fifth centuries. Hun in this connection means a vandal. In history, **Vandals** were a Germanic people who raided Roman provinces in the third and fourth centuries AD before devastating Gaul (406–409), conquering Spain and North Africa and sacking Rome. They were finally crushed by Belisarius at Carthage in AD 535. To vandalise means to engage in wanton and deliberate destruction of people and property. To say of someone that he is a vandal means that he is a menace to society and must be restrained at all costs.

Shoah A Hebrew word for holocaust meaning 'destruction'. It refers specifically to the six million Jews who were murdered by the Nazis.

Churban The destruction of the Temple or Bet Hamikdash (the holy house), first by the Babylonians in 586 BC and again by the Romans in AD 70. *Churban* is another name for holocaust.

Chuppa The canopy under which a marriage is performed. The wedding ceremony is distinct from the celebration. The bridegroom breaks a glass which has been placed under his foot, as a reminder of the destruction of the Temple.

Wailing Wall A wall in Jerusalem, the last remaining part of the Temple of Herod, held sacred by Jews as a place of prayer and pilgrimage; it is also called the **Western Wall**. Pious Jews sometimes place a **kvittel** in the Wall. This is a special plea to the Almighty, which they hope will receive His attention.

Mikvah is a pool used by Jewish women for ritual purification after their monthly period.

Midrash A homily on a scriptual passage derived by traditional Jewish exegetical methods and consisting usually of embellishment of the scriptural narrative. One of a number of such collections of homilies composed between 400–1200. In Hebrew it means 'commentary'.

Judas or **Judas Iscariot** was the apostle who betrayed Jesus to his enemies for thirty pieces of silver. The name is now applied to anyone who betrays a friend. It also denotes a bird or animal used to lure others of their kind to slaughter. The word is sometimes used for a peephole or a very small window in a door. In the seventeenth century when Catholics in Britain were being persecuted, Judas holes were made in Catholic houses where priests could hide. When Judas hanged himself on a tree, this became known as a Judas tree.

Maariv The Hebrew name for evening prayer, whilst **Mincha** is the word for afternoon prayers; sometimes in winter the two services are combined, and said together.

Midas In Greek legend he was a king of Phrygia, who had the power to transform everything he touched into gold. When we speak of somebody who is very successful in business, we say 'he has the Midas touch.'

Milk round still means a route along which a milkman regularly delivers milk and various other food products, but it defines also a regular series of visits made by recruitment officers from industry and commerce to universities to obtain the services of the best students.

Hobson's Choice The choice of taking what is offered or nothing at all. It refers to Thomas Hobson (1544–1631), an English liveryman who gave his customers no choice – they had to take the nearest horse; if they did not they received none. 'Take it or leave it.'

Lock, Stock and Barrel means completely, entirely.

Nail 'On the nail' means to pay immediately. 'To be as hard as nails' means to be without sentiment or feeling. 'To hit the nail' means to reach the target; 'to hit the nail on the head', means to have judged correctly.

Luftwaffe was the German Air Force, literally meaning 'air weapon'.

Blitzkrieg A swift military attack with the object of quickly overcoming the enemy. In German it means 'lightning war'.

Wehrmacht The armed services of the German Third Reich from 1935–1945. In German it means 'defence force'.

Reich The holy Roman Empire was the first Reich and the Hohenzollern Empire from 1871–1919 was the Second Reich. This was followed by the Weimar Republic (1919–1933) and then the Nazi dictatorship (1933–1945): the Third Reich. In German the word means 'kingdom'.

Pyrrhic Pyrrhus, king of Epirus, defeated the Romans at the battle of Asculum in 279 BC but sustained such heavy losses that it was not really a victory. A Pyrrhic victory is considered now to be of doubtful value – the price exacted in gaining it was not worth it.

Rommeln is a new word in German, meaning to move at a tremendously fast rate. It is named after the German Field Marshal, Erwin Rommel (1891–1944). Rommel, nicknamed 'the Desert Fox', was noted for his brilliant generalship in North Africa during World War II. He later committed suicide in France, after the officers' plot against Hitler had failed.

A **Stalag** was a prisoner of war camp in Germany in World War II for non-commissioned officers and other ranks. It is short for *Stammlager* which in German means 'basecamp'.

Condottiere A soldier in a professional mercenary company in Europe from the thirteenth to the sixteenth centuries. It is an Italian word meaning 'leadership'.

Chapter 26

What's in a name?

Stalin, Joseph (1879–1933) was a Georgian, whose original name was Joseph Vissarionovich Dzugashvili. All through his life he spoke with a Georgian accent. He realised that his name would be an immense drawback to his political career. He became general secretary of the Communist Party of the Soviet Union as it was then called. Subsequently, he succeeded Lenin as head of the party and created a totalitarian state, crushing all opposition, especially in the great purges of 1934–1937.

The purge began after the assassination of Kirov, a member of the Politburo. There is strong reason for believing that this was done by Stalin, in order to give him the pretext for his next action. Bukharin and Rykov, members of the Politburo, were arrested and brought to trial. They confessed to having committed the most atrocious crimes, such as poisoning wells, and to having acted as spies for Japan. Kremlinologists, people who study developments and actions in the Soviet Union, have been puzzled over these confessions, and how they were psychologically possible.

Stalin had maintained the conviction that it was possible to build Socialism in Russia, despite the fact that it was economically backward in comparison with the advanced capitalist countries. He instituted a system of collective and State farming and persecuted farmers whom he called *kulaks* – '*kulak*' is the Russian word for 'fist'. Thousands of these *kulaks* had their farms seized, and they themselves were driven out, and exiled to Siberia. Large numbers died on the route, victims of hunger, cold and disease.

Stalin had appointed as public prosecutor André Vyshinksky (1883–1952). He had been a member of the Menshevik Party, rivals to the Bolsheviks (Communists), and in his eagerness to show that he was more

Catholic than the Pope, he conducted the case against the fallen leader with unabated zeal. He was rewarded for this, being made Foreign Minister (1949–1953) and Soviet representative at the United Nations.

Stalin had clashed with Leon Trotsky (1879–1940), whose original name was Davidovich Lev Bronstein. Trotsky was a leading Communist theorist. He was a leader of the November Revolution (1917) and as Commissar of foreign affairs and war (1917–1924) brilliant creator of the Red Army. He was ousted by Stalin after Lenin's death and had to flee from Russia to Mexico in 1929. In 1940 Stalin sent an agent there, who murdered him. Trotsky was famous for his theory, called Trotskyism, in which he called for immediate world-wide revolution by the working class. The Trotskyist International was developed from the international federation of anti-Stalin Communists founded in 1936.

Commissar was originally a Russian word meaning an official of the Communist Party responsible for political education, especially in the armed forces. **Commissariat** is derived from Commissar, and was a Government department before 1948. It is now called a Ministry and is in charge of food supplies and equipment in general.

KGB (abbreviation) The Soviet secret police since 1954. It was based along the lines of the Committee of Public Safety set up by the Jacobins to consolidate their rule during the French Revolution. This Committee however only operated in France – its function was solely to support the Revolution – it was not for export. The Soviet KGB operates on a worldwide scale, and indulges in all kinds of activities, economic and political. In this it resembles the **CIA** (Central Intelligence Agency) in the USA. It is a US bureau created in 1947 to co-ordinate and conduct espionage activities wherever possible, but especially in the States of Southern America.

The **Gestapo** (German secret police) in the Nazi regime was different. It was concerned with actions in Germany and was notorious for its brutal methods of interrogation.

Chapter 27

Blatt A Russian and Jewish word to describe activities forbidden by law. If for example the Government has imposed rationing on the population, be it on food, clothing, or other items, the demand for such items is so great, that the general public will buy them, accepting that it is illegal. This is similar to what happened in the USA when Prohibition by the Government was introduced. There it was known as bootlegging, and it was conducted on so vast a scale that the USA Government was forced to withdraw the ban. It is impossible to enforce the law when the vast majority of the public is opposed to it.

Ulpan A special school set up in Israel to teach Jews from many nationalities, speaking different languages, to acquire a knowledge of Hebrew as rapidly as possible, All instruction is in Hebrew and the methods employed are similar to those applied by the Berlitz School of Languages.

Parev A dish containing neither meat nor milk products and so fit for use with either meat or milk dishes. Eating milk and meat dishes together is **treif**. In Israel such dishes would not be served in any hotel or restaurant.

Milchik is a milk dish; **Fleishik** is a meat one.

Kosher The name applied to food which has been prepared in accordance with Jewish religious law. It now has a more general meaning. To say, for instance: 'This is not kosher,' would be to describe a scheme or proposition that is not acceptable, and conversely if it is acceptable. *Kosher*/not *kosher* also carries with it the hint of legality/illegality.

Kashrut The condition for being fit for ritual use in general; the system of dietary laws which require ritual slaughter; the removal of excess blood from meat; the complete separation of milk and meat; and prohibition of such foods as pork or shellfish. The word actually means 'fitness' in Hebrew.

Halacha A Jewish religious law. A ruling on some specific matter, and that part of the Talmud concerned with legal matters apart from homiletics. It may be compared with **Aggadah** which is a homiletic passage from the Talmud. Collectively, the homiletic part of traditional Jewish literature, as contrasted with Halacha, consists of elaboration on the Biblical narrative or tales from the lives of ancient Rabbis and any traditional homiletic interpretation of scripture.

Tanach The Hebrew Bible as used by Jews, divided into Torah, Prophets and Hagiographia.

Pentateuch The first five books of the Old Testament regarded as a unity.

Koran The sacred book of the Moslems, believed by them to be the infallible word of God dictated to Mohammed through the arch-angel Gabriel. In Arabic the word means 'reading a book'.

Pitta A flat, round slightly leavened bread with a hollow inside like a pocket, which can be filled with food. It is called Arab or Greek bread and it comes chiefly from the Middle East. In Greek it means 'cake'.

Parfait A rich, frozen dessert made from eggs and cream, with ice-cream and fruit. In French it means 'perfect'.

Pariah A social outcast, a member of a low caste in South India. At festivals pariahs were allowed to be drummers, and in Tamil they are actually called drummers.

Shechina The radiance in which God's imminent presence in the midst of His people, especially in the Temple, is visibly manifested. The divine presence is contrasted with the divine transcendence. In Hebrew it means 'to dwell'.

Shofar A horn sounded daily in the synagogue during the month of Elul and repeatedly on Rosh Hashanah, and used by the ancient Israelite as a warning summons. In Hebrew the word means 'a ram's horn'.

Cognoscenti People with informed appreciation of a particular field, especially the fine arts. In Italian it means 'to learn about'.

Compère A master of ceremonies who introduces cabaret and television acts. In French it actually means 'godfather'.

Cabaret A floor show of dancing, singing or other entertainment at a nightclub or restaurant. The word derives from Norman-French meaning 'tavern'.

Spook A ghost, or a person masquerading as one, haunting a particular domicile, which could be called a spooky house. In Dutch it means 'ghost'.

Masquerade A party or gathering where the guests wear masks and costumes. It could also be a pretence or disguise with the object of dissembling. In Spanish it means 'mask'.

Camouflage The exploitation of natural surroundings or artificial aids to conceal or disguise the presence of military persons with or without their equipment; it also applies to animals who try to escape predators, animal or human, by absorbing themselves into the coloration of their surroundings. In French it means to disguise or deceive.

Écraseur A surgical device, consisting of a heavy wire loop placed around that part of the body which has to be removed and tightened till it cuts through. In French it means to crush. This brings to mind the famous saying of Voltaire (1694–1780): *'Écrasez l'infame'* (crush the infamous thing).

Sansculottes During the French Revolution this meant a revolutionary of the poorer classes having extreme republican sympathies who wore pantaloons or trousers rather than knee breeches. In French it means 'without knee breeches'.

Pasteurisation was called after Pasteur (1822–1895). Louis Pasteur was a French chemist and bacteriologist. He discovered that the fermentation of milk and alcohol was caused by micro-organisms. The process of pasteurisation removed this. He also devised methods of immunisation against anthrax and rabies and pioneered stereo chemistry.

Glitzen Showily attractive or flashy. In German it means to glitter.

Cobbler If Jews had a caste system, the lowest person in that system would probably be a cobbler. The Jewish expression: 'It's gone down the cobblers' street,' means that things have degenerated a great deal. Some of this derogation has rubbed off into English:
   'This is a load of old cobblers,' means that whatever it is, it is a load of rubbish and unworthy of consideration.

Ritzy is applied to any expensive or luxurious hotel. It takes its name from César Ritz (1850–1918). To put on the Ritz means to make an ostentatious display. 'This isn't the Ritz,' means that the hotel is shabby and ill-equipped.

Naughty nineties refers to Britain in the period 1890–1899 which was considered to be a period of fun-loving and laxity, especially in sexual morals.

Form is a word with contrary meanings: We may say, 'He is on form,' meaning 'he is performing well'. 'He has form,' would mean to police officers that he had committed crime.

Bold has several meanings.
   1. courageous and ready to take risks
   2. immodest or impudent
   3. conspicuous or outstanding

Bola A missile used by cowboys and Indians of South America. It consists of two or more heavy balls on a cord. This is hurled at a running animal, such as an ox or emu, so as to entangle its legs. In Spanish it means 'ball'.

Lay aside is an example of a word with contrary meanings.
   a. to abandon or reject
   b. to store or reserve for future use

Chapter 28

An agreeable example of the convergence of ethnicity is afforded by the case of Alsace-Lorraine (The French names for Elsass-Lothringen (German).) For a long historical period France had endeavoured to annexe the provinces, which had been a part of Germany before Germany became a Reich. The leading kingdom (there were a number of kingdoms including Bavaria and Saxony) was Prussia. In the Franco-Prussian War, in which the French were defeated, Alsace-Lorraine reverted to Prussia as Elsass Lothringen. The change did not much affect the population. The Germans living in it had not been persecuted or harassed by the French, nor had the French been persecuted by the Germans. The two groups lived in harmony and there were never any riots or disturbances as the mixed population adjusted itself to the change of regime. This showed that in civilised countries the convergence of ethnicity could be peaceably achieved.

The results of the divergence of ethnicity have been starkly shown at the present time in Yugoslavia, where a process of 'ethnic cleansing' is taking place. 'Ethnic cleansing' leads inevitably to the expulsion and destruction of the weaker group – it is genocide. It is a horrible evil, whose tentacles spreading far and wide are awakening similar manifestations in neighbouring lands.

Pale The phrase 'beyond the pale' means an action or situation which transcends the limits of social acceptance. The phrase derives from the Pale of Settlement in Tsarist Russia. At that time Jews were not allowed to live freely in all Russian cities; they were restricted to a particular area called the Pale of Settlement. They could leave it only by government permission, though they found a possible way out: the **nachalnik** (official in charge) could be bribed (**chabar**).

Pale-face A word used by North American-Indians to describe the white population.

Pommie A mildly offensive word used by Australians and New Zealanders to describe an English person. It derives from POME; acronym for Prisoner of Mother England, referring to convicts.

Wallaby A member of the International Rugby Union football team of Australia.

Komsomol The youth association of the Soviet Union, for boys and girls aged 14–20. In Russian it means the 'Communist Party of Youth'.

Decembrist A participant in the unsuccessful revolt in December 1825 by Russian officers to unseat the Tsar, Nicholas I (1825–1855).

It is interesting to note that the proposals for reforms which would benefit the Russians excluded Jews, who were to be deported to the inhospitable wastes of Asia. Many would die on the road – the survivors would perish at their destination. How endemic is this Russian anti-Semitism?

Kremlin Twelfth century citadel in Moscow containing the former Imperial Palace, three Cathedrals and the offices of the Soviet government. **Kremlinologist** is the name given to one who studies and analyses the policies and practices of the Soviet Government. In Russian, the word *Kremlin* means fort or citadel.

Agitprop A Bureau of the Central Committee of the Communist Party of the Soviet Union in charge of agitation and propaganda on behalf of Communism. It is the promotion, as in the arts, of political propaganda, especially of a Communist nature. In Russian it means 'agitation and propaganda'.

The hundred days: in French history this was the period between Napoleon's arrival in Paris from Elba and his subsequent abdication (20 March–29 June 1815).
    The hundred years' war was between England and France and began in 1340. The war was not continuous but intermittent. Despite early victories, the English were finally defeated and expelled from the whole of France with the exception of Calais, which they finally lost in 1558. Mary

Tudor, Queen of England, known as Bloody Mary for her religious persecution, was said to have died saying: 'You will find Calais written on my heart.'

Goulash A rich stew originating in Hungary, made of beef, veal or lamb, highly seasoned with paprika. The term is also used in card games such as bridge, when the cards are dealt without being shuffled, to produce freak hands.

Gourmand A person too strongly interested in food and drink. A **gourmet** is one who has cultivated a discriminating palate for the enjoyment of good food and drink. Both terms were originally French.

Jezebel According to the Old Testament, she was the wife of King Ahab of Israel. She fostered the worship of Baal and tried to destroy the prophets of Israel, using cruel and vindictive means to do so. Nowadays a Jezebel is a woman who will stoop to any means to accomplish her desires, irrespective of how this might affect others.

Doxy has two contrary meanings.
1. Opinion or doctrine, especially concerning religious matters.
2. A prostitute.

The latter derives from Dutch where it means 'doll'. In the first case it can be used in the expressions, 'orthodoxy' or 'heterodoxy'.

Yeshivah A traditional Jewish school or theological college devoted to the study of Rabbinic literature and the Talmud. It also provides instruction for children of elementary school age in both religious and secular subjects.
  In Hebrew it means 'a seat'.

Mitzvah A commandment or precept, especially one found in the Bible – a good deed. To emphasise the importance of an action or deed one says: 'If you do this, you are doing a real Mitzvah.' In Hebrew it means 'a commandment'.

Pasquinade An abusive lampoon or satire, especially one posted in a public place. It was the name given to a Roman statue disinterred in 1501, which was annually posted with satirical verses in Italian.

Lampoon A satire in prose or verse ridiculing a person or literary work. In French it is used as a refrain in a drinking song.

Wallah A person in charge of a special task or duty. In Hindu it means 'protector'.

Khedive The viceroy of Egypt under Suzerainty (1857–1914). In Persian it means 'prince'.

Pahlavi the Middle Persian language, especially used in classical Zoroastrian and Manichean literature.

Palaver tedious and time-consuming business, especially when of a formal nature; loud and confused activity and talk; a hubbub, and a humorous interpretation as a conference: Palaver is sometimes used as a means of persuasion and flattery. It can also mean an argument, or trouble arising from the argument. In Portuguese it means 'talk'.

Paper the house has two meanings
1. to replace wallpaper in a house, and putting up new wallpaper.
2. in theatrical terms, giving away a free ticket.

Chapter 29

An outstanding example of where language became a factor of political divergence is afforded by Russia. In the nineteenth century especially, the Russian aristocracy used French instead of Russian. We can note this in Tolstoy's great work *War and Peace*, which is replete with French.

Russian is also distinguished from other European languages (apart from Latin) by not having a word for 'a' and 'the' (demonstrative adjective). The Russians can only say, for instance, 'I have book', which could mean, 'I have a book,' or 'I have the book'; they cannot emphasise *the* book, when they wish to do so. The lack of a word for 'the' has been clearly shown in the political sphere with regard to the problems in the Middle East. There the Israelis are in dispute with the Arabs with regard to territories occupied by them (the Israelis). The Russians cannot talk about '*the* occupied territories'; they can only talk about 'occupied territories', and this brings confusion in its train. It is surprising, in view of these circumstances, that the Russian Academy of Languages has not dealt with this problem by introducing an appropriate word. When the Bolsheviks came to power in 1917, they eliminated several letters in the Russian alphabet, which were duplicates of other letters. This can be seen when comparing literary works before 1917 with those written afterwards.

It is interesting to note the Russian word for Sunday. We have taken 'Sunday' from the Norse: the day of the sun. In Russian, Sunday is the day of resurrection.

Tolstoy – actually meaning fat – Count Lev Nicholaevich (1828–1910) was a Russian novelist, short-story writer, and philosopher; he was the author of two monumental works: *War and Peace* (1865–1869) and *Anna Karenina* (1865–1877). Tolstoy said that he was by nature a sinful person consumed by lust. He tells of the spiritual crises he underwent to restrain his sexual passion for his cook. As a result of these crises he began a deep study of the New Testament and elaborated the principles which it preached. The most important principle he accepted was Christianity, based on the doctrine of non-resistance to evil. 'The meek shall inherit the earth,' but even if they did not and inherited nothing, they should not be envious towards those who were rich and powerful. 'Turn the other cheek!' It is not surprising that Marxists in reply coined the phrase: 'Religion is the opium of the people.'

This was part of the attitude of Karl Marx (1818–83) and Friedrich Engel (1820–1895). Together they wrote the Communist Manifesto in 1848, the year of Revolutions in Europe. 'A spectre is haunting Europe,' and it has been so for nearly 150 years, until the recent collapse of the Soviet Union.

In *Das Kapital* Marx developed his theories of the class struggle and the economics of capitalism. He was one of the founders of the First International Working Men's Association. He held, with Engels, that actions and human institutions are economically determined, that the class struggle is the basic agent of historical change and that the capitalist system would ultimately be superseded by communism.

Thesis — the capitalist class
Antithesis — the working class
Synthesis — the classless society

Marx's thesis of class struggle was not accepted by the Arab leader, Nasser Gamel Abda (1918–1970), Egyptian soldier and statesman, and President of Egypt. He was one of the leaders of the Coup that deposed King Farouk in 1952 and he became premier in 1954, when he displaced General Neguib. In reply to actions by Western Powers, including the USA, he nationalised the Suez Canal which, under International Law, was an international waterway, open to all nations whether in peace or war. This provoked an international crisis and Britain and France sent military forces to the Canal. Israel also did so, moving with lightning speed and speedily reaching the Canal. The American President Eisenhower was furious, and ordered the British and French to withdraw, which they did, and so did Israel.

Nasser was now seen by all the Arab States in the Middle East as the leader they had been looking for, to enable them to destroy Israel. In 1967 Arab armies converged from all sides on Israel, but the latter replied with lightning attacks which tore their enemies into shreds. The war lasted only six days, and is described as the Six Day War.

Zionism A political movement for the establishment and support of a national homeland for Jews in Palestine, as it was then called. It is now mainly concerned with the development of the modern State of Israel and fostering the return to it from Jews in the Diaspora. The founder of the Zionist movement was Dr Theodore Herzl, an Austrian-Jewish journalist who had been in Paris at the time of the Dreyfus affair and the violent anti-Semitism it engendered in France. Herzl was deeply shocked by this. If this could happen in France, no Jews were safe anywhere. The only solution was to establish a *Judenstaat* (Jewish State) in Palestine. He said in 1898 that this could take place within five or fifty years, and it was in fact established in 1948. 'If you will it, it is no dream,' he declared.

Diaspora The dispersion of the Jews after the Babylonian and Roman conquests of Palestine. It is also the name given to the Jewish communities outside Israel. In the New Testament it refers to the body of Christians living outside Palestine. In Greek it means 'a scattering'.

Mahatma In Hindustani a Brahmin sage; in theosophy an adept.

Maharajah Any of various Indian princes; especially those of the former native states. In Hindu it means 'great'. **Maharani** is the wife of a Maharajah.

Maharishi A Hindu teacher of religious and mystical knowledge.

Mahdi The title assumed by Mohammed Ahmed (1843–1885), a Sudanese military leader who led a revolt against Egypt and captured Khartoum in 1885. Also one of a number of Muslim messiahs expected to convert forcibly all non-Muslim people to Islam. In Arabic, *Mahdi* is 'one who is great'.

Messiah The awaited king of the Jews, to be sent by God to free them; he is also considered as an exceptional hoped-for liberator of a country and people. The Christian considers the Messiah has already come in the form of Jesus Christ. In Hebrew the word means 'one who is anointed'.

Sephardi A Jew of Spanish, Portuguese, or North African descent or, loosely, any Oriental Jew; it is also the pronunciation of Hebrew by them, and as spoken in Israel. In Hebrew it means 'southerner'.

Ashkenazi A Jew of German or East European descent and the pronunciation of Hebrew by these Jews; a descendant of Noah through Japhet and hence taken to be identified with the ancient Ascanians of Phrygia and, in the medieval period, with the Germans.

Vikings Scandinavians who raided by sea most of North and West Europe from the eighth to the eleventh centuries, later often settling in parts of Britain; the term applies to any sea rover, plunderer or pirate. From old Norse: 'a sea-inlet'.

Sepoy A Hindu soldier in the service of the British. From the Portuguese *sepoy* meaning 'soldier'. The Sepoy Rebellion or Mutiny relates to the Indian mutiny of 1857–1858.

Draco A Greek statesman and lawmaker in the seventh century BC, whose laws were so severe that the death penalty was prescribed for nearly all types of offence. A Draconian sentence means that it is exceptionally severe.

Minotaur In Greek mythology, a monster with the head of a bull and the body of a man. It was kept in the labyrinths of Crete, and it fed on human flesh until it was destroyed by Theseus. It stems from the Greek meaning 'a bulk'.

Thalassocracy The Government of a nation having dominion over large expanses of the seas. In Greek, *thalassa* means 'sea'.

Rubicon A stream in Italy in ancient times marking the boundary between Italy and Cisalpine Gaul. In 49 BC Julius Caesar led his armies across and marched on Rome. He broke the law that a general might not lead his army out of the province in which he was posted and so committed himself to war with the Senatorial Party. This meant that he had reached the point of no return. To cross the Rubicon means to commit oneself irrevocably to some definite course of action. 'To burn one's boats' has much the same meaning.

Chapter 30

We have previously discussed instances of civil war. In India, the movement by the indigenous population took a much less radical line. This could be explained by the fact that there were two political groups – one Hindi and one Moslem.

The respective leaders were Mohamdas Gandhi (1869–1948), called the Mahatma, for the Hindus; and Jawaharlal Nehru (1889–1964) for the Moslems.

Gandhi had been an advocate in South Africa, but not been able to accept the domination of the Whites over the Coloureds and he left the country and went to India. He played a major part in India's struggle for home rule. From the very start, he made it abundantly clear that he was entirely indisposed to use violence; he advocated that passive resistance plus an anti-British economic policy would give results.

Many of his followers would lie down on railway tracks, and so impede movement. The engine drivers, both British and Hindu, could not bring themselves to drive over prostrate bodies. Whether this policy would have been successful against Russians, Germans or Spaniards is highly doubtful.

In 1883 the Russian General Skobelev, who had distinguished himself in the Russo-Turkish War of 1877, became Governor General of Turkmenistan. He immediately executed 3,000 of the inhabitants, saying that this would show them that they could not trifle with Imperial Russia.

Gandhi advocated a policy of boycott of British goods, especially cotton. The British cotton industry had had a considerable export trade with India, but this now shrank. He advocated that Indians should wear loincloths, as he himself did. He was frequently imprisoned by the British for organising acts of civil disobedience. He urged hunger strikes as a means of achieving reform; he also campaigned for the Untouchables and attempted to unite Moslems and Hindus.

Left-wing elements in Britain stated that they thought British policy was 'divide and rule'. How false this was, was shown when in 1947 the country was divided into India and Pakistan. No matter how carefully this was done, the result was inevitable that there should be numbers of Indians in Pakistan, and numbers of Pakistanis in India. There was a great deal of bloodshed before the frontiers were agreed.

The result was that Pakistan now consisted of West and East Pakistan and both parts were surrounded by large swathes of Indian territory. Indian pressure on East Pakistan resulted in this territory breaking away from West Pakistan, and calling itself Bangladesh, after the civil war there, and the defeat of Pakistan by India. Whether the Hindus really gained from this is, from the economic point of view, very doubtful. Bangladesh is a very poor country and cannot avoid being a drain on India's resources; these are very meagre, as India itself is a poor country which receives £600 million a year from Britain and large quantities of food from the USA.

During the Cold War period India also received substantial aid from the one-time Soviet Union; the latter's collapse has certainly not aided India.

The province of Kashmir has been a bone of contention between India and Pakistan since 1947. The north-west part of the country is held by Pakistan and is known as Azadkashmir. In 1956 the remainder was incorporated into India as the state of Jammu Kashmir; it is a fruit-growing and cattle-grazing area.

Gandhi continued with his policy of hunger strikes and non-cooperation until he was murdered by a fanatic in 1948.

In general, it could not be maintained that the British were a ruthless colonial power. During the several centuries when they governed the country there has been only one revolt – the Indian Mutiny; with this exception, large scale repression did not take place until Amritsar in 1919. Amritsar is a city in India, in the North-West Punjab, and is the centre of the Sikh religion. In 1919 numbers of unarmed supporters of Indian self-government were massacred by British troops. The British commander had panicked and lost control of the situation. He was recalled home and severely punished.

The Sikhs have a Golden Temple in Amritsar. In 1984 they quarrelled with the Indian Government and used the temple as a military base. Mrs Indira Gandhi, Prime Minister of India at this time, sent in forces to subdue the Sikhs and eject them. Mrs Gandhi had several Sikhs in her bodyguard, and they assassinated her.

Ganef A thief, or someone who engages in sharp practice and is unscrupulous. In Hebrew or Yiddish it means 'a thief'.

Gansey A jersey or pullover. From Yiddish.

Babu A title. A person could describe himself, say, as John Babu Smith or Babu John Smith. In Hindi it means 'father'.

Gateau Any of various elaborate cakes, usually layered with cream and richly decorated. From the French: 'cake'.

Geronimo-Apache Redskin leader who led a campaign against the white settlers, until he was captured by them in 1886. Nowadays his name is used as a shout by American paratroopers as they jump into battle.

Negus A title of the Emperor of Ethiopia.

Éclat A brilliant or conspicuous success or a showy display; ostentation; an achievement which receives an enthusiastic approval. From the French '*éclater*', to burst.

Éclair A finger-shaped cake of choice pastry, usually filled with cream and covered with chocolate. In French it means 'lightning' because it does not last long.

Laissez-Faire individualism is the doctrine of unrestricted freedom in commerce for private interests with no interference by government. A tragic example of this doctrine was the Irish famine in the 1840s when the potato crop failed. The government refused to supply food or any aid. This was not because they were hard-hearted and indifferent to suffering, but because it would be against the doctrine. One result of this was a mass emigration of Irish people to the USA. They left with a burning hatred of Britain, and this has to a large extent remained to this day. Thus the IRA (Irish Republican Army), with its campaign of terrorism against Britain, receives considerable support from Irish Americans.

The doctrine of *laissez-faire* is receiving less and less credence in European countries. There it is accepted that government must participate in the economic life of the community by having a mixed economy, and whenever necessary it must 'prime the pump' or kick-start it.

Laissez-passer is a document granting unrestricted access or movement to the holder.

Carte blanche was a document sealed with the Royal seal and which bore no names. The holder of this document had unlimited power and if he filled in the name of any person, whoever he or she might be, that person could be arrested and imprisoned without being brought to trial. The Bastille was the prison where many people over the years were incarcerated and died there in this way. In modern times the expression has gained a new significance. For instance, if we say the government has sent representatives to a conference and given them *carte blanche*, we mean it has given them authority to negotiate freely.

Carte de jour A menu listing dishes available on a particular day.

Cartel A collective international association of independent enterprises, formed to monopolise production and distribution of a product or service, and to control prices. A good example of a cartel was formed by a group of oil-producing States in the Middle East in the seventies. They trebled the price which consumers paid and they had to pay the extra. In politics 'cartel' means an alliance of parties to further common aims. In Britain this could mean an agreement by the Labour and Liberal Democratic Parties on certain issues. From French and Italian – a written challenge.

Mien A person's manner, bearing, or demeanour, expressing personality or mood. From the French, where it means 'aspect'.

Mig Any of various Soviet Union fighter aircraft, from the names of its designers Mikoyan and Giuevich.

Palanquin A covered litter used in the Orient, carried on the shoulders of four men. From the Portuguese: 'couch'.

Pizza A dish of Italian origin consisting of a baked dish covered with cheese and tomatoes, usually with the addition of mushrooms, anchovies, sausage or ham. It comes from the Italian.

Roll up has two different and contradictory meanings:
  1. an invitation for people to come to a meeting or conference to help and participate.

2. Roll up – the map of Europe; it will not be wanted for the next ten years: the famous phrase used by William Pitt when in 1805 Napoleon defeated the combined Russian and Austrian armies at Austerlitz, a town in Moravia in central Czechoslovakia.

Run through has two meanings:
1. to examine carefully a document or documents, or a plan of action to be undertaken by an individual or group of people – the documents are to be returned and carefully held.
2. to kill a person with something sharp: e.g., 'He ran his opponent through.'

Khaki A dull yellowish-brown colour; a hard-wearing fabric of this colour used as uniforms by British troops. In Persian, 'khaki' means 'dust'.

Mufti has two meanings:
1. civilian dress worn by a person who normally wears a military uniform.
2. a Moslem legal expert and adviser on the law of the Koran.

In the former Ottoman Empire, the leader of the religious community. The Grand Mufti of Jerusalem was the acknowledged chief leader, similar to the Archbishop of Canterbury, and the Chief Rabbi of the British Commonwealth. Before the second world war, the Grand Mufti of Jerusalem was a warm supporter of the German Nazis and their policy of the annihilation of all Jewry.

Muezzin The official of a Mosque who calls the faithful to prayer five times a day from the minaret.

Minaret A slender tower of a Mosque having one or more balconies from which the Muezzin calls the faithful to prayer. From the Arabic meaning 'lamb'.

Jihad A holy war by Moslems against the infidels. In Arabic it means 'conflict'.

Infidel In normal English, an infidel is a person who has no religious beliefs whatsoever, but to Moslems, Christians are still infidels. To the Moslems, believers in other religions are in the same category as unbelievers.

Muesli A mixture of rolled oats, nuts and fruit, eaten with milk. From the German *'musl'*.

Purée A smooth thick pulp of cooked and sieved fruit, vegetables, meat or fish. From the French: 'to purify'.

Purdah The custom in some Hindu and Moslem communities of keeping women in seclusion; they wear clothing that conceals them completely when they go out. It is also a screen in Hindu households used to keep women out of view. In addition it is a veil worn by Hindu women of high caste. In Hindu it means 'veil'.

Parashah Any of the sections of the Torah read in the synagogue and any of the subsections of the weekly lessons read on Sabbath. In Hebrew it means 'to divide'.

Sheva Brachot The seven blessings said during the marriage service and repeated at the celebration afterwards, and any of the celebratory meals held on the seven days after a wedding.

Shibboleth The use of language that acts as a test of belonging to, or as a stumbling block to becoming a member of a particular social class or profession. In the Old Testament, the word is used by the Tribe of Gileadites as a test word for the tribe of Ephraimites. This is somewhat similar to the Chinese who cannot pronounce the letter r: 'very' as 'velly' and, when one says, 'I eat rice,' it sounds as if he was saying, 'I eat lice.' In Hebrew, Shibboleth is 'an ear of grain'.

Shadchan A Jewish marriage broker, who arranges marriages. This is its exact meaning in Hebrew.

Shidduch An arranged marriage; this also means any negotiated agreement between two sides. 'It's a *shidduch*,' is a phrase to indicate this.

Altogether is another word with two contradictory meanings:
1. We are altogether agreed.
2. 'We are in the altogether' means we are naked.

Blarney Flattering talk, to cajole with flattery, wheedle; one who has kissed the Blarney stone – a stone in Blarney Castle in the south-west

Republic of Ireland. Anyone who has kissed the stone is said to be endowed thereby with great persuasive skill. 'Don't give me any of your blarney' is a phrase used to express this, or 'He's kissed the Blarney Stone.'

Blasé To become indifferent to somebody or something because of familiarity or surfeit. It indicates boredom or a lack of enthusiasm. From the French *blaser*, to cloy.

Gremlin A term first used by the Royal Air Force (RAF) during the Second World War and implying an imaginary imp jokingly said to be responsible for mechanical trouble in aircraft. It is now applied to describe any breakdown or failure.
When these take place, we say 'the gremlins are at it'.

Rickshaw a small two-passenger vehicle, drawn by one or two men and used in parts of Asia. There is a similar vehicle called a *Trishaw*; it has three wheels, and is propelled by a man peddling, as on a tricycle.

Ricochet When a bullet rebounds from a surface with a characteristic whining or zipping sound; it also describes the motion or sound of a rebounding object. From the French. Origin not known.

Robe de Chambre A dressing gown. From the French.

Squaw An offensive description of a North American Indian woman or wife. It comes from the Algonquian language, meaning a female creature. One could say that squaw is onomatopoeic; it has the authentic sound. Squaw man is a derogatory term for a white or non-Indian man married to a North American Indian woman.

Synagogue A building for Jewish religious service and instruction, where Jews congregate for religious study.

Golem In Jewish legend, an artificially created human being brought to life by supernatural means. Nowadays it has acquired another meaning: a Golem means someone who is very stupid. To say of someone, 'He is a golem,' is a very derogatory remark.

Coup d'état A brilliant and successful political action.

Coup de foudre A sudden and amazing action or event – literally 'a lightning flash'.

Coup de grace A mortal or finishing blow delivered by someone to his opponent. Sometimes it is given as an act of mercy to one who is suffering. In French it is described as an 'act of mercy'.

Knesset The unicameral Parliament of Israel. Formerly it meant, with *Beth*, a place of study and worship.

Knapsack A canvas or leather bag, strapped on the back and carried by a soldier. From the Dutch, to bite or snap.

Barmitzvah A term applied to a Jewish boy who has reached the age of thirteen and is considered now able to fulfil all religious obligations; it is also the occasion, ceremony or celebration of that event, the boy himself on that day. In Hebrew it means 'son of the law'. In Liberal and Reform synagogues, girls can become batmitzvah (daughter of the law) at the age of twelve.

Minyan The number of persons required to be present for religious services; it must be at least ten males. In orthodox synagogues females will not be acceptable if there are not ten males; in this case the service will be adjusted.

Rabbi In Judaism, a man qualified (in accordance with traditional religious law) to expand, teach, and rule in accordance with this law; he is the leader of a congregation, the minister of a synagogue. The Rabbis were the early Jewish scholars, whose teachings are recorded in the Talmud. In Liberal religious circles women are accepted as Rabbis and are addressed as such. The wife of an Orthodox Rabbi is a rebbetzin.

Rebbe Usually the dynastic leader of a Chassidic sect. There are several such dynasties in the United States, mostly in New York, and they are bitterly opposed to each other. There have been brawls between them which have required the intervention of the police to suppress them.

Chassid A member of a sect of Jewish mystics founded about 1750 in Poland, characterised by religious zeal, and a spirit of prayer, joy and charity. Such a sect had been formed in the second century BC to combat

Hellenism. The Chassid believes fervently in the power of the Rabbi. To be permitted to eat at the Rabbi's table was to him the acme of bliss. The founder of this sect is known as Baal Shem Tov (master of the good name).

Gubbah A long, loose outer garment worn by Moslems, men and women, especially in India.

Fuselage The word stems from Arabic and means the main body of an aircraft excluding the wings and tailplane. From the French *fuseler* – to shape like a spindle.

Fustian is another word with double meaning:
1. a hard-wearing fabric of cotton mixed with flax or wool with a slight nap – useful.
2. cheap or worthless, useless

It also means pompous and bombastic.

Fuss is another word with double meaning:
1. they made a fuss over the new baby, showing love and affection for it.
2. they made a fuss over the bill, meaning a complaint or objection.

Esprit de Corps A consciousness of, and pride in, belonging to a particular group – the sense of shared purpose and fellowship. From the French.

Espresso A strong coffee made by forcing steam or boiling water through ground coffee beans, or an apparatus for making coffee in this way. From the Italian: 'pressed coffee'.

Eyewash has two meanings:
1. a mild solution used for applying to the eyes for relief of irritation.
2. this is rubbish or nonsense. It is possible that the mild solution has been ineffective and thus equated as useless rubbish. It is possible that remedies for eye troubles may be introduced; if so, the word 'eyewash' would begin to lose its stigma.

Cartoon A humorous or satirical drawing in a newspaper or magazine concerning a topical event; a sequence of drawings in a newspaper or on television relating a comic or adventurous situation. It is also a full-size preparatory sketch for a fresco, tapestry, or mosaic from which the final work is copied or traced. From the Italian *cartone*, meaning 'pasteboard'.

Carton A cardboard box for containing goods, or a container of waxed paper or plastic, in which liquids such as milk are sold. Also from the Italian *cartone*.

Doge Chief magistrate in the republic of Venice until 1797 and Genoa until 1805. From the Italian.

Surveillance Close observation or supervision maintained over a person or group, especially if he or they are in police custody. From the French *surveiller*, to watch.

Sang-froid Complete composure and self-possession. From the French, literally: 'cold blood'.

Sucrose The technical name for sugar. From the French *sucre* –'sugar'.

Soupçon A slight amount of a food or drink added to the course. From the French – 'a dash'.

Pince-nez Eyeglasses that are held in place only by a clip over the bridge of the nose. From the French, literally: 'pinch-nose'.

Palliasse A straw-filled mattress or pallet. From the French.

Marianne Female figure personifying the French Republic after the Revolution of 1789, wearing a Phrygian cap. This was a conical cap of soft material worn in ancient times which became a symbol of liberty during the French Revolution.

Bocage Wooded countryside characteristic of Northern France with small irregular-shaped fields and many hedges and copses, or woodland scenery represented in ceramics. From the French.

Gibraltar A limestone promontory at the tip of Southern Spain. In Arabic it is called *Gebeltarik* after the Arabic general Tarik who captured it in 1711. It was taken by Spain in 1462, who ceded it to Britain in the

Treaty of Utrecht in 1713. They have been claiming it strongly at the present time.

Shiah One of the two main branches of Islam, now mainly in Iran, which regards Mohammed's cousin Ali and his successors as the true Imam and another name for Shiite, characteristic of this sect, or its beliefs and practices.

Imam A leader of prayer in a mosque and leader of a Moslem community; it is also a honorific title applied to eminent doctors of Islam, such as the founders of orthodox schools. He may be any of a succession of either seven or twelve religious leaders of the Shiites and regarded by them as being divinely inspired. From the Arabic meaning 'leader'.

Ayatollah One of a class of Iranian Shiite leaders. From the Arabic, meaning 'sign of God'.

Fatwa A decree or order given by an Ayatollah which must be obeyed by his followers, even if the order is to take place in a foreign country in defiance of the laws of that land. It is some years now since the Ayatollah Khomeini issued a *fatwa* against Salman Rushdie who had written a book which was considered by him to be derogatory to the Moslem religion.

Sunni One of the two main branches of orthodox Islam, consisting of those who acknowledge the authority of the Sunna. It is a less common word for Sunnite.

Doppelganger A ghostly duplicate of a living figure. From the German, meaning 'double-goer'.

Achilles heel In Greek mythology, Achilles was the son of the god Peleus and the sea-goddess Thetis. He was one of the foremost Greek warriors at the siege of Troy. When he was a baby, his mother plunged him into the river Styx. (In Greek mytholoy the Styx was a river in Hades across which the boatman Charon ferried the souls of the dead. In the Greek, Styx means 'hate'.) This action by her was to make his body invulnerable, except for the heel by which she held him. At the Trojan War he was killed by being struck in the heel. Thus, it means a fatal weakness. One might say of a plan that it was unsound, as it had an Achilles heel, and thus would fail.

Nosh To eat tasty tit-bits in small quantities. From the Yiddish.

Blunt has two contrary meanings:
1. 'His speech is blunt', meaning sharp and to the point.
2. 'His knife is blunt'; it will not cut; it will have to be sharpened.

Poniard A small dagger with a slender blade. From the French meaning 'dagger'.

Écarté A card game for two with 32 cards and king high, it also applies to ballet and describes a body position in which one arm and the same leg are extended at the side of the body. From the French *écarter*, to discard.

Barbecue A meal cooked out of doors over an open fire, or an outdoor party or picnic at which this meal is served. It also means to cook meat or fish on a grill, usually over charcoal and often with a highly seasoned sauce. From the Spanish *barbacoa*.

Kebab A dish consisting of small pieces of meat, tomatoes and onions, threaded onto skewers and generally grilled over charcoal. From Arabic, meaning 'roast meat'.

Vizier A high official in certain Moslem countries, especially in the former Ottoman Empire. A vizier served in various capacities, such as provincial governor or as chief minister to the Sultan. From the Arabic, meaning 'to bear a burden'.

Karate A traditional Japanese system of unarmed combat, employing smashes, chops and kicks made with the hands, feet, elbows or legs. In Japanese it means 'empty hand'.

Entente cordiale A friendly understanding between powers. It was especially prominent in the relationship before and during the First World War beween France and Britain.

The relationship has weakened since then, and today it is not an outstanding feature.

Bomb has two meanings:

1. The conference went like a bomb, i.e., everything went off well.

2. The bomb went off at the conference, meaning that there was destruction and possibly injury or death to people there.

Marathon This word referred originally to the feat of the messenger who ran twenty-six miles from Marathon to Athens to bring the news of the victory in 490 BC of the Greeks over the Persians. It is now an event in Modern Olympics, and it also indicates a long or arduous task or assignment. A marathon effort means a tremendous effort.

Sparta An ancient Greek city in the Southern Peloponnese, famous for the discipline of military prowess and its citizens, and for their austere way of life. To say, 'He leads a Spartan life,' means he is very frugal.

Stentor In Greek mythology, a man with an extremely powerful voice who died after he lost a shouting match with Hermes, the herald of the gods. To say, 'He spoke in stentorian tones,' means he spoke with a very powerful voice.

Pontiff A former title of the pagan high priest of Rome, later used of popes and occasionally of bishops but now used exclusively of the Pope. From the French *pontife*.

Champignon Any of various edible mushrooms. In French it means 'unattested chalice', a drinking cup or goblet. In Catholic churches it is a golden or silver cup containing the wine at Mass; it also means a cup-shaped flower. From the French: 'a cup'.

Hierophant In ancient Greece, an official high priest of religious mysteries; also a person who interprets and explains esoteric mysteries. From the Greek: 'one who reveals'.

Marzipan A paste made from ground almonds, sugar and egg whites, used to coat fruit cakes or moulded into sweets. From the French.

Mardi-Gras The festival of Shrove Tuesday, celebrated with great revelry. In French: 'fat Tuesday'.

Matza A brittle, very thin, biscuit of unleavened bread, traditionally eaten at Passover. It commemorates the departure of the Israelites from Egypt, when they had no time to leaven the bread.

Diatribe A bitter or violent criticism or attack. From the Greek: 'discourse'.

Abigail In the Old Testament, the woman who brought provisions to David and his followers, and subsequently became his wife. In later times, the meaning degenerated to 'a lady's maid': a humble person.

Chapter 31

Gay now has two meanings:
1. 'He is gay' meaning that he is cheerful and happy.
2. 'He is gay', meaning that he is a homosexual.

This second meaning has practically obliterated the first. No one now uses it in its first meaning.

Crop Two meanings:
1. 'We have had a good crop', meaning a good harvest and that we have increased our food supplies.
2. 'We crop our hair'; we have reduced our hair – we have had a haircut.

Rule out Two meanings:
1. To rule out: to disregard and discard.
2. to rule out a route: to examine carefully how to get from A to B.

Rub off Two meanings:
1. Will this stain rub off? (be erased).
2. Will his ability rub off on me? Will I obtain some of his ability?

Loco To be insane, but also 'in place'. *In loco parentis*: in the position of parent.

Concierge A caretaker of a block of flats or hotel, who lives on the premises. From the French meaning 'servant'.

Enceinte Meaning pregnant, and also a boundary wall enclosing a defended area. From the French; to encompass.

Kamerad German for 'comrade', but generally used by German soldiers as a shout of surrender in wartime.

Rodomontade Boastful words or behaviour and bragging. From the French, 'boasting'.

Pierrot A male character from French pantomime with a whitened face, white costume, and pointed hat. From the French meaning 'clown'.

Quai d'Orsay The quay along the southern bank of the Seine, Paris, where the Foreign Office is situated. To quote the Quai d'Orsay means that this is what the Foreign Office says.

Swastika Originally a primitive religious symbol or ornament in the shape of a Greek cross, usually having the arms bent at right angles in a clockwise or anti-clockwise direction. It was officially adopted in 1935 by Nazi Germany as its emblem. From Sanskrit, meaning 'prosperity'.

Aryan In Nazi ideology, a Caucasian of non-Jewish descent, of the Nordic type; a member of any of the peoples descended from the Indo-Europeans. A speaker of an Irian or Indic language in ancient times relating to, or characteristic of, an Aryan. From the Sanskrit, meaning 'of noble birth'.

Crescendo In music, a gradual increase in loudness; or the musical direction or symbol indicating this – the symbol is written over the music affected. From the Italian: 'increasing'.

Maftir The final section of the weekly Torah reading or the person by whom it is read, who also reads the Hafthorah.

Magen David In Yiddish, another name for the Star of David.

Yom Kippur Annual Jewish holy day, a day of fasting on which prayers of penitence are offered in the synagogue throughout the day; it is also called the Day of Atonement.

Rosh Hashanah The festival marking the Jewish New Year, celebrated on the first and second day of Tishri and marked by penitential prayer and the blowing of the Shofar. In Hebrew it means 'beginning of the New Year'.

Sublime Porte The court or government of the Ottoman Empire. From the French meaning 'high gate'.

Kaddish An ancient Jewish prayer largely written in Aramaic and used in various forms in separate sections of the liturgy. Mourners recite some of these during the year after and on the anniversary of a death.

Cabbala An ancient Jewish mystical tradition based on an esoteric interpretation of the Old Testament; any secret or occult doctrine of science. In Hebrew it means 'tradition'.

Guru In Hindi a religious leader or teacher who gives personal spiritual guidance to his disciples; a leader or chief theoretician of a movement; weighty.

Sheikh In Moslem lands the head of an Arab tribe or village; a venerable old man; a religious leader or high priest. In Arabic it means 'old man'.

Shekel Any of several former coins and units of weight of the Near East, nowadays also the currency unit in Israel.

Absinthe A potent green alcoholic drink, technically a gin, with high wormwood content. In French it means 'wormwood'.

Accolade Strong praise or approval; the ceremonial gesture used to confer knighthood, originally an embrace, now a touch on the shoulder with a sword. From the French, meaning 'to hug'.

Entourage A group of attendants or retainers who surround an important person as a retinue. It also means surroundings or environment. From the French *entourer*, to surround.

Strafe To bombard from the air enemy troops, installations and important areas. During the World Wars the Germans had a phrase: '*Gott strafe England*' – May God punish England. In German, *strafe* means 'punishment'.

Burnous A long circular cloak with a hood attached, worn by Arabs.

Oracle A prophecy, often obscure or allegorical, revealed through the medium of a priest or priestess at a shrine. It is also an agency through which a prophecy is transmitted, or any person or object believed to indicate future action with infallible authority, It was the holy of holies in the Israelite Temple. Oracles are another term for Scripture. In ancient times the Oracle of Delphi was believed to have these powers. Nowadays one might say of a person: 'He is an Oracle,' meaning he knows a great deal, and one can confidently consult him with reference to a proposed line of future action.

Sanction Final permission or authorisation, aid or encouragement. Sometimes a principle that imparts binding force to a rule or oath. It is also a penalty laid down in a law for contravention of its principles; it is also a coercive measure, especially one taken by one or more states against another guilty of violating international law. It can also be said to give authority.

We have recently seen that the United Nations has confirmed sanctions against Saddam Hussein, dictator of Iraq, and against Serbia in the present civil war in former Yugoslavia. Sanctions would be far more effective than they are today if all nations supported them. Unfortunately some nations indulge in sanction-busting for a short-term profit.

Rapporteur A person appointed by a committee to prepare reports of meetings or to carry out an investigation. From French: 'a reporter'.

Rapprochement A resumption of friendly relations especially between two countries. From French, meaning 'bringing closer'.

Rascal has two meanings:
1. a disreputable person, a villain.
2. an affectionate or mildly reproaching term for a child or old man.

From French, meaning 'rabble'. **Rapscallion** has a similar meaning.

Jargon a specialised language concerned with a particular subject, culture or profession; a language characterised by pretentious syntax, vocabulary or meaning. It also means gibberish or pidgin: to use or speak in jargon. From the French *gargouille*, throat.

Imbroglio a confused or perplexing political or interpersonal situation. From the Italian *imbrogliare*, to confess.

Sauerbraten Beef marinated in vinegar, sugar and seasonings and then braised. From the German meaning 'sour roast'.

Sauerkraut A finely shredded and pickled cabbage. From the German: 'sour cabbage'.

Armageddon Actually a city in Northern Palestine, as it then was – a site of so many battles in the Old Testament that its name has become a synonym for fierce and destructive conflicts. In the New Testament it is viewed as the final battle at the end of the world between the forces of good and evil. Armageddon means War!

Petit bourgeois A section of the middle class with the lowest social status, generally of shopkeepers and lower clerical staff; a member of this stratum. A characteristic indicating a sense of self-righteousness and a high degree of conformity to established standards of behaviour.

Petit four Any of various very small rich sweet cakes and biscuits, usually decorated with fancy icing, jam or marzipan. From the French: 'a small oven'.

Petite Of a woman, small, delicate and dainty. From the French: 'small'.

Coleslaw A salad of shredded cabbage, mayonnaise, carrots and onion. From the Dutch: 'cabbage salad'.

Espadrille A light shoe with canvas upper, especially with a braided cord sole. From the French diminutive of esparto, which is used for the soles of such shoes.

Espalier An ornamental shrub or fruit tree that has been trained to grow flat, as against a wall; the trellis, framework or arrangement of stakes on which such plants are trained. From the French, meaning 'trellis'.

Petits pois Small sweet fresh green peas. From French: 'small peas'.

Petit mal A mild form of epilepsy characterised by periods of impairment or loss of consciousness for some seconds. From the French: 'little illness'.

Perestroika From the Russian, meaning a massive reconstruction and rebuilding of industrial complexes, system of Government and political institutions.

Glasnost A Russian word meaning clarity and clearness.

Solidarnosc A Polish word meaning 'solidarity', which has recently come to the fore in Poland.

Bon marché A French word meaning 'cheap'.

Bon mot A clever and fitting remark. French, literally: 'good word'.

Maghreb North-west African Arab States: Morocco, Algeria, Tunisia, Libya. In Arabic: the West.

Magi The Zoroastrian priests of the ancient Medes and Persians; the magi from the East, who came to do homage to the infant Jesus.

Khamsin A southerly wind in the Middle East from about March to May. In Arabic it means 'fifty'.

Diet 1. a food programme to control weight
2. the assembly of the estates of the holy Roman Empire

Abacus A Russian counting device that consists of a frame holding rods on which a specific number of beads are free to move. Each rod designates a given denomination such as units, tens and hundreds.

Ikon A representation of Christ, the Virgin Mary or a Saint, especially one painted in oil on a wooden panel, depicted in a traditional Byzantine style and venerated in the Eastern Church. From the Russian: 'image'.

Patriarch The male head of a tribe or family. A very old or venerable man. In the Old Testament, any of the three ancestors of the Hebrew people, Abraham, Isaac and Jacob. Also any of Jacob's twelve sons, the ancestors of the twelve tribes of Israel. In the early Christian Church, the bishop of one of several principal sees, especially those of Rome, Antioch and Alexandria. In Eastern Christianity the head of the Coptic, Armenian, Syrian, Jacobite or Nestorian Churches, and of certain other non-Orthodox Churches in the East; also the oldest or most venerable member of a group community etc; he is also regarded as the founder of a community tradition.

Marrano a Spanish or Portuguese Jew of the late Middle Ages who was converted to Christianity, especially one forcibly converted, but secretly adhering to Judaism. From the Spanish meaning 'pig', with reference to the Jewish prohibition of eating pork.

Matador The principal bull-fighter who has to kill the bull. It is also a game played with dominoes. In Spanish, *matar* means 'to kill'.

Toreador A bull fighter. In Spanish: one who takes part in bull-fighting.

Pis aller As a last resort or stopgap. From the French: 'at the worst going'.

Pilgrim A person who undertakes a journey to a sacred place as an act of religious devotion. The pilgrimage to Canterbury was famous in previous centuries. From the French *pèlerin*.

Porte cochère A large covered entrance for vehicles leading into a courtyard; a large rock projecting over a drive to shelter travellers entering or leaving vehicles. From the French; 'carriage entrance'.

Retsina A Greek wine flavoured with resin.

Levant A former name for the area of the eastern Mediterranean now occupied by Lebanon, Syria and Israel. From the French *lever*, to rise (of the sun).

Ladino A language of Sephardi Jews based on Spanish with some Hebrew elements and usually written in Hebrew characters. Also called Judeo-Spanish.

Polder A stretch of land reclaimed from the sea or a lake especially in the Netherlands. From the Dutch *polse*.

Basilica A Roman building used for public administration, having a large rectangular central nave, with an apse on each side, and an apse at the end – a rectangle; early Christian or medieval churches usually having a nave with clerestories, two or four aisles, and one or more vaulted apses with a timber roof; a Roman Catholic Church having special ceremonial rights. From the Greek, meaning 'of a king'.

Quadrille A square dance of five couples; a piece of music for such a dance, alternating between simple duple and compound duple time. From the Spanish: a diminuative of *quadro*, 'four'.

Cordon bleu The sky-blue ribbon worn by the highest members of knighthood under the Bourbon monarchy; a knight entitled to wear it. It also denotes food prepared to a very high standard. From the French, meaning 'blue ribbon'.

Cordon sanitaire A guarded line serving to cut off an infected area of a nation from infiltration or attack. The Poles erected such a cordon in 1921 to protect them against possible attack by the Red Army.

Compote A dish of fruit stewed with sugar or in a syrup served hot or cold. From the French.

Caprice A sudden and unpredicted change of attitude to behaviour; a tendency to such changes. From the French.

Boyar A member of an old order of Russian nobility, ranking immediately below the princes, abolished by Peter the Great. A title from old Russian.

Arrondissement In France, the largest administrative sub-division of a *département*; a principal *département* of large cities. From the French *arronder*, to make round.

Cou-cou A preparation of boiled corn meal and okra stirred to a stiff consistency with a cou-cou stick; eaten in the West Indies.

Conquistador An adventurer or conqueror, with special reference to the Spanish conquerors of the new world in the sixteenth century. From the Spanish: 'conqueror'.

Admiral The supreme commander of a fleet or navy. From the Arabic *amiramual al farn*: commander of the sea.

Inca A member of a South American Indian people whose great empire centred on Peru and lasted from about 1100 AD to the Spanish conquest in the 1530s; the ruler of the empire, and the language of the Incas. From the Spanish, meaning 'king'.

Hyksos A member of a nomadic Asian people who controlled Egypt from about 1720 BC to 1560 BC. From the Egyptian: 'ruler of the lands of the nomads'.

Commando An amphibian military unit trained for raids. From Afrikaans.

Anthropophagi Cannibals; from the Greek.

Schuss A straight high speed downhill run. From the German, meaning 'shot'.

Schutzstaffel The German SS. A paramilitary organisation within the Nazi party that provided Hitler's bodyguard, security forces including the Gestapo, concentration camp guards and a corps of combat troops (the Waffen SS) in World War II. In German: 'a protection guard'.

Gestapo Secret state police of Nazi Germany (from *Geheimstatspolitzei*).

Valkyrie A Norse myth: any of the beautiful maidens who served Odin, the supreme god. The divinity of wisdom, culture, war and the dead. The Valkyries rode over the battlefields to claim the dead heroes and take them to Valhalla.

Valhalla The great hall of Odin, where warriors who die in battle as heroes, dwell eternally.

Cantina A bar or wine shop in a Spanish speaking country.

Canton Any of the 22 political divisions of Switzerland. A sub-division of a French *arrondissment*. From French, meaning 'a corner'.

Delicatessen Various foods already cooked and prepared, or a shop selling such foods. From the German, literally: 'delicacies'; often shortened to 'deli'.

Pâtisserie A shop where fancy pastries are sold. From the French *pâtissier*, a pastry cook.

Kindergarten A class or small school for young children to prepare them for primary education. From the German, literally: 'children's garden'.

Chaise longue A long low chair for reclining, with a back and single arm rest. From the French: 'long chair'.

Legate A messenger, envoy or delegate; in the Roman Catholic Church, an emissary to a foreign state, representing the Pope. From the French: 'a deputy'.

Mandarin In the Chinese Empire a member of the nine senior grades of the bureaucracy, entered by examination: a high-ranking official with extensive powers and thought to be outside political control. Mandarin Chinese has been the official language of China since 1917; it is the form of Chinese spoken by about two-thirds of the population and taught in schools throughout China. From Malay, meaning 'councillor'.

Tundra a vast treeless zone lying between the ice-cap and the timber line of North America and Eurasia, and having a permanently frozen subsoil. From the Russian: 'hill'.

Steppe An extensive grassy plain without trees. In Russian: 'lowland'.

Pasha A provincial governor or other high official of the Ottoman Empire or the modern Egyptian kingdom, placed after a name when used as a title; a *pashalik* is the province of a pasha.

Bey In the Ottoman Empire, a title given to senior officers, provincial governors, and certain other officials or nobles.

Alcalde In Spain and Spanish America the commander of a castle or fortress, or the governor of a prison; the mayor or chief magistrate of a town. From the Spanish: 'a judge'.

Burgomaster The Chief Magistrate of a town in Germany, Austria, Belgium or Netherlands. From the German and Dutch.

Guerilla A member of an irregular armed force that fights an occupying power. It also combats strong regular forces of the government of its own country and this is called guerilla warfare. From the Spanish meaning 'a little war'.

Kukri A knife with a curved blade that broadens towards the point, especially used by Gurkhas. From the Hindi.

Kudos Indicating acclaim, glory or prestige. From the Greek. In modern Turkey a title of address corresponding to Mr.

Kasha A dish originating in Eastern Europe, consisting of boiled or baked buckwheat. From Russian: 'buckwheat'.

Würst A large sausage, especially popular in Germany and Austria. From the German, literally: 'rolled'.

Pétillant Spoken of wine which is slightly effervescent. From the French: 'effervescent'.

Cadi A judge in a Moslem community. From the Arabic: 'judge'.

Kohen A member of the priestly family of the tribe of Levi, descended from Aaron, who has certain ritual privileges in the synagogue service. From Hebrew, meaning: 'priest'.

Kohen Gadol The high priest.

Levi A descendant of the tribe of Levi, who has certain privileges in the synagogue service.

Shema The central statement of Jewish belief. 'Hear O Israel, the Lord is your God – the Lord is one.' In Hebrew, literally: 'hear'.

Volte-face A reversal of opinion or policy; a change of position, so as to look or lie in the opposite direction. From the French: a turning.

Marchesa Marchioness, wife or widow of a Marquis. From the Italian.

Cotillon A French formation dance of the eighteenth century.

Jonah In the Old Testament, a Hebrew prophet who had been thrown overboard from a ship in which he was travelling, who was swallowed by a whale and vomited on to dry land. Nowadays, a Jonah is considered to bring bad luck to those around him.

Jinx Another name for a Jonah.

Mafia An international secret criminal organisation originating in Italy, but which has become very powerful in the United States. In Italian, it means 'hostility to the law' – a *mafioso* means a person belonging to the Mafia.

Ski One of a pair of wood or metal runners that are used for gliding over snow. Skis are commonly attached to shoes, but may also be used as landing gear for aircraft. From the Norwegian: 'snowshoe'.

Soufflé A very light fluffy dish made with egg yolks and stiffly beaten egg whites, combined with cheese and fish; a similar sweet or savoury cold dish set with gelatine made light and puffy by beating and cooking. From the French *souffler*, to blow.

Pâté A spread of very finely minced liver, poultry or fish served usually as an hors d'oeuvre. A savoury pie of meat or fish. From the French: 'paste'.

Kreplach A small filled dough casing usually served in soup. From the Yiddish.

Paprika A mild powdered seasoning made from a sweet variety of red pepper; the fruit or plant from which the seasoning is obtained. From the Serbian *paper*, 'pepper'.

Mish-mash A confused collection or mixture. From the Yiddish.

Tattoo is a signal by drum or bugle ordering soldiers to return to their barracks, or a military display or pageant, taking place usually at night. From the Dutch *taptoe*.

Another definition is to make pictures or designs on the skin, by pricking or staining with indelible colours; a design made by this process; the practice of tattooing. From Tahitian: 'tattoo'.

Tabu or **Taboo** Forbidden or disapproved; placed under a social prohibition or ban. In Polynesia and other islands of the South Pacific, tabu means marked off, as being sacred and forbidden; any prohibition resulting from social or other conventions; ritual restriction or prohibition of something that is considered holy or unclean. From the Tongan.

Smorgåsbord A variety of hot or cold savoury dishes, such as pâté or smoked salmon served in Scandinavia, as hors d'oeuvre or as a buffet meal. From the Swedish: 'sandwich table'.

Smørrebrod Small open savoury sandwiches served as hors d'oeuvres especially in Denmark. In Danish it means butter bread.

Calibre The diameter of a cylindrical body, especially the internal diameter of a tube or the bore of a firearm. It also means ability or distinction. From the French.

Minion A favourite or dependent especially a fawning or servile one. It also means dainty or pretty. From the French *mignon*, dainty.

Machismo A strong or exaggerated masculine pride or masculinity. From Spanish *macho*, male.

Maisonette Self-contained living accommodation often occupying two floors of a large house and having its own outside entrance. From the French: a diminutive of 'house'.

Maître d'Hôtel Head waiter or steward; the manager or owner of a hotel.

Maigre Not containing flesh and so permissible as food, on days of religious abstinence. From the French meaning 'thin'.

Majlis The Parliament of Iran. In various South African and Middle East countries 'an assembly'. From the Persian: 'assembly'.

Major Domo The chief steward or butler of a great house. From the Spanish *mayordomo* meaning 'head of the household'.

Bashibazouk In the nineteeenth century, one of a group of irregular Turkish soldiers notorious for their brutality. In Turkish: 'a corrupt head'.

Schnapps A Dutch spirit distilled from potatoes; in Germany any strong drink. From the German, meaning 'to snap'.

Schnitzel A thin slice of meat, especially veal. In German, 'cutlet' from *schnitzen*, to carve. A Wiener schnitzel is a Viennese cutlet and very highly prized.

Paella A Spanish dish made from rice, shellfish, chicken and vegetables; also the large flat frying pan in which a paella is cooked.

Kümmel A German liqueur flavoured with aniseed and cumin.

Kumiss A drink made from fermented mare's milk, drunk by certain Asian tribes, especially in Russia, also used for medicinal purposes. From the Russian *kumys*.

Kaaba A cube-shaped building in Mecca – the most sacred Moslem pilgrim shrine – into which is built the black stone (Kaaba stone) which Moslems believe was given by the angel Gabriel to Abraham. Moslems turn in its direction when praying. In Arabic, *Kaaba* is a cube.

Mecca A city in Saudi Arabia, birthplace of Mohammed, the holiest city of Islam. It is used nowadays of something or somebody that draws immense attention. If we say, 'He is the mecca of all eyes,' it means that he is the centre of attraction.

Medina A city in Saudi Arabia; the second most holy city of Islam, with the tomb of Mohammed. *Medina* is also the ancient quarter of any of various north African cities. In Arabic, literally: 'a town'.

Meshuga Mad. From Yiddish.

Bratwürst A type of small pork sausage. From the German.

Apprehend has two meanings:
1. to arrest, or take into custody
2. to understand or grasp mentally

Calvary The place outside the walls of Jerusalem where Christ was crucified. Now used to express any experience which involves great suffering.

Sharia The doctrine that regulates the lives of Moslems.

Shampoo A liquid or cream preparation of soap or detergent to wash the face. From the Hindi *champo*, to knead.

Cri de coeur A cry from the heart – a sincere appeal.

Kasbah The citadel of various North African cities; the quarter where a *kasbah* is located. From the Arabic *kasby*, a citadel.

Khan A title borne by medieval Chinese emperors and Mongol and Turkish rulers – it is usually added to a name, such as Kublai Khan, a title of respect borne by important people in Afghanistan and Central Asia. From the Turkish: 'ruler'.

Caravanserai In some Eastern countries a large inn enclosing a courtyard, providing accommodation for caravans. From the Persian *caravan*: 'inn'.

Pimiento A Spanish pepper with a red fruit used raw in salads, cooked as a vegetable and as a stuffing for green olives.

Souk In the Middle East, an open-air market place. From the Arabic: 'a market place'.

Katzen jammer A confused uproar; a hangover; from the German: 'wailing'.

Shtick A comedian's routine or act. From the Yiddish meaning 'a piece'.

Picket A small detachment of troops or warships positioned towards the enemy to give early warning of attack. Also an individual or group that stands outside an establishment to make a protest or dissuade or prevent employees and clients from entering. From the French *piquer*, to sting.

Maquis The French underground movement that fought against the German occupying forces in World War II; a member of this movement. From the French: 'thicket'.

Maquette A sculptor's small preliminary mould or sketch. From the French: 'a small sketch'.

Maquillage make-up or the application of make-up.

Marabout A Moslem holy man or hermit in North Africa; a shrine of the grave of a *marabout*. From the Arabic *mourabit*.

Planchette A heart-shaped board on wheels with a pencil attached which writes messages under supposed spirit guidance. From the French: 'little board'.

Couchette A bed or berth in a railway carriage that can be converted from seats. From the French: diminutive of *couche*, a bed.

Pirouette A body spin, especially in dancing, on the toes or ball of the foot; to perform a pirouette. From the French meaning 'a spinning top'.

Carbine A light automatic or semi-automatic rifle of limited range. Also a *carabiniere* or an Italian national policeman.

Bersagliere A member of a rifle regiment in the Italian army. From Italian *bersaglio*, a target.

Montagnard A member of a North American Indian people living in the North Rocky Mountains. From the French: 'a mountaineeer'.

Autostrada An Italian motorway.

Stiletto A small dagger with a slender tapered blade; a sharply pointed tool used to make holes in leather or cloth. A stiletto heel is a very high heel on a woman's shoe, tapering to a very narrow base. From the Italian *stilo*, a dagger.

Staccato Music whose notes are short, clipped, and separate. Used as a musical direction: 'In a *staccato* manner'. From the Italian *staccare*, to detach.

Schmaltz Excessive sentimentality especially in music; animal fat used in cooking. From the German and Yiddish: 'melted fat'.

Pianissimo A piece of music to be played very quietly. From the Italian: superlative of *piano*, soft.

Millefleurs A design of stylised floral pattern, used in textiles and tapestries. From French: 'a thousand flowers'.

Festschrift A collection of essays or learned papers contributed by a number of people to honour any eminent scholar. From the German: 'celebration writing'.

Hamburger A flat brown smoked sausage made of finely minced pork or beef, often served in a bread roll.

Fortissimo In music, a very loud passage. From the Italian: 'very strong'.

Clairvoyant Having great insight or second sight. From the French.

Montage The art or process of composing pictures by the superimposition of miscellaneous elements, such as other pictures or photographs. From the French *monter*, to mount.

Cheroot A cigar with both ends cut off separately. From Tamil: 'curl' or 'roll'.

Bureau A writing desk; a chest of drawers; an official or agency, especially one providing services for the public; a Government Department. From the French: 'desk' or 'office'.

Rendezvous A meeting or appointment to meet at a specified time and place; a place where people meet. From the French: 'present yourself'.

Camarilla A group of confidential advisers to the Spanish king. In Spanish: literally, 'a little room'.

Garage A building used to house motor vehicles; an establishment in which motor vehicles are repaired or serviced. From the French: 'to protect'.

Götterdämmerung A German myth, the twilight of the gods: their ultimate destruction in a battle with the forces of evil. The Norse equivalent is **Ragnarok**.

Tref Food ritually unfit to be eaten. In Hebrew, it means an animal which has been torn.

Ratatouille A vegetable casserole made of tomatoes, peppers and aubergines, fried in oil and stewed slowly. From the French *touiller*, to stir.

Kris A Malayan and Indonesian stabbing or slashing knife with a scalloped edge.

Kaftan A long coat-like garment usually worn with a belt and made of rich fabric, worn in the East. An imitation of this, worn especially by women in the West, consists of a loose dress, with long wide sleeves. From the Turkish.

Aide-mémoire A memorandum or summary of the items of an agreement. From the French: 'to aid memory'.

Aide de camp A military officer serving as personal assistant to a senior. From French: 'camp assistant'.

Writing on the wall This phrase refers to Belshazar. In the Old Testament he was son of Nabonidus, and co-regent of Babylon with his father for eight years. At a feast, he received a divine message of doom written on a wall. Nowadays 'the writing is on the wall' means that something disastrous or even fatal may befall one.

Beluga A large white sturgeon of the Black and Caspian Seas; a source of caviar and isinglass. Also another name for white whale. From Russian, meaning 'white'.

Lunette Anything that is shaped like a crescent; an oval or circular opening to admit light to a dome; a semi-circular panel, containing a mural or sculpture. It is also called *lune*. In the Roman Catholic church it is a case fitted with a bracket to hold the consecrated host. From the French: 'crescent'.

Reconnaissance The process of obtaining information about the position, resources and activities of an enemy or potential enemy; the act or process of reconnoitring. From the French: 'to explore'.

Plateau A wide mainly level area of elevated land; a relatively long period of stability; a levelling off. From the French: 'something flat'.

Parsee An adherent of a monotheistic religion of Zoroastrian origin. The adherents of this religion were driven out of Persia by the Moslems in the eighth century AD. It is now found chiefly in Western India. From Persian: a Persian **Pharisee** (a member of an ancient Jewish sect opposed to the Sadducees). Nowadays they have the reputation of being self-righteous or hypocritical persons.
From the Aramaic: 'separated'.

Necropolis A burial site or cemetery. From the Greek, meaning 'dead'.

Kabaka Any of the former rulers of the Baganda people of South Buganda.

Corvette A lightly armed escort warship. From the Dutch *corf*, a basket.

Corsair A pirate, especially on the Barbary Coast. From French, *corsaire*, a pirate.

Abattoir Another name for slaughterhouse. From the French: 'to fell'.

Lebensraum A territory claimed by a state on the grounds that it needs it in order to survive or grow. Hitler made such a claim on Russia, saying that if he had the Urals, the Germans would be swimming in fat. In German, literally: 'living space'.

Lehr A long tunnel-shaped oven used for annealing gas. From the German 'pattern'.

Romany Another name for a gypsy; the language of the gypsies belonging to the Indu branch of the Indo-European family but incorporating extensive borrowings from local European languages. From the Sanskrit *domba*, man of a low caste of musicians, of Dravidian origin.

Dravidian A family of languages in South and Central India and Sri Lanka, including Tamil, Malaysian, Telugu and Kannada; a member of one of the aboriginal races of India.

Kletter Schuh A lightweight climbing boot with a canvas or suede upper and felt or cord sole. From the German: 'climbing shoe'.

Kneidel A small dumpling usually served in chicken soup. From the Yiddish.

Rondeau A poem consisting of ten or thirteen lines with two rhyming and having the opening word of the line used as an unrhymed refrain. From the French *rondel*, a little round.

Shamanism The religion of some peoples of Northern Asia, based on the belief that the world is pervaded by good and evil spirits, who can be influenced or controlled only by the Shaman. From the Sanskrit *shama*, a religious exercise.

Fanfarronade Boasting or flaunting behaviour. To boast comes from the French *boasiler*.

Braggadacio Vain, empty, boasting; a person who boasts. From the Italian.

Bordello A brothel. From the Italian.

Huguenot A French Calvinist designating the French Protestant church.

Hugues Surname of Genevan burgomaster in the sixteenth century.

Hippopotamus From the Greek: 'a river horse'.

Sherpa A member of a people of Mongolian origin living on the southern slopes of the Himalayas in Nepal, noted as mountaineers.

Negligée A woman's light dressing gown, especially one that is lace-trimmed; any informal attire. From the French *negliger*, to neglect.

Yarl A Scandinavian chieftain or noble. From Norse.

Doukhobor A member of a Russian sect of Christians that originated in the eighteenth century. In the early nineteenth century a large minority emigrated to Canada. From the Russian.

Dukhoborcy Spirit wrestler, from *Dukh*, 'spirit wrestler'.

Ukaze In Imperial Russia, an edict of the Tsar. From the Russian *ukazat*, to command.

Vodka An alcoholic Russian drink made from grain or potatoes and usually consisting only of water and rectified spirit. In Russian, it is a diminutive of *voda*, water.

Valise A small overnight travelling bag. From the French.

Portmanteau A large travelling case made of leather, especially one hinged at the back so as to open out into two compartments. From the French: 'cloak carrier'.

Timbre A distinctive tone quality differentiating one vowel or sound from another. From the French: 'note of a bell'.

Trompe An apparatus for supplying the blast of air in a forge, consisting of a thin column, down which water falls, drawing in air from side openings.
From the French, literally: 'trumpet'.

Trommel A revolving cylindrical sieve used to screen crushed minerals. From the German: 'a drum'.

Spek South African bacon fat, or fatty pork used for larding venison or other game. From Afrikaans.

Sirocco A hot, oppressive and often dusty wind, usually occurring in spring, beginning in North Africa and reaching Southern Europe; any hot southerly wind especially one moving to a low pressure centre. From Arabic: 'east wind'.

Lama A priest or monk of Lamaism, which is the Mahayana form of Buddhism in Mongolia and Tibet.

Dalai Lama Until 1959 the chief lama and ruler of Tibet. He was born in 1955 and was the fourteenth holder of this office, but fled to India in 1959, when the Chinese invaded and occupied Tibet. From the Mongolian *dalai*, ocean.

Chogyai The title of the ruler of Sikkim.

Chevrette The skin of a young goat or the leather made from the skin. From the French: 'kid'.

Chevron Militarily, a badge or insignia consisting of one or more V-shaped stripes, to indicate a non-commissioned rank or length of service; in heraldry, an inverted V-shaped charge on a shield; any V-shaped pattern or device.

Chez At the home of; with, among, or in the manner of. From the French.

Chili con Carne A highly seasoned Mexican dish of meat, onions, beans and chilli powder. From the Spanish: chilli with meat.

Casque A helmet or a helmet-like processor structure. From the French.

Cassata An ice-cream originating from Italy, usually containing nuts and candied fruit.

Catafalque A temporary raised platform on which a body lies in state before or during a funeral. From the Italian *catafalco*.

Chemin de fer A gambling game, a variation of baccarat. From the French: 'railway'.

Baccarat A card game in which two or more punters gamble against the banker. From the French.

Cloche A bell-shaped cover used to protect plants; a woman's almost brimless, close fitting hat, typical of the 1920s and 1930s.

Tequila A spirit that is distilled in Mexico from the agave plant, and which forms the basis of many mixed drinks. From Mexican Spanish.

Sepulchre A burial vault, tomb or grave. From the French *sepulcre*.

Malfeasance The doing of a wrongful or illegal act, especially by a public official. From the French *mal faisant*.

Maffick To celebrate publicly and extravagantly; the rejoicing of the British at the relief of the town of Mafeking in 1900 during the Boer War.

Croissant A French flaky crescent-shaped bread roll made of a yeast dough similar to puff pastry.

Dauphin From 1349–1830, the title of the direct heir to the French throne – the eldest son of the King of France. **Dauphine**: wife of the Dauphin.

Gendarme A member of the police force in France or in countries formerly controlled by France.

Mésalliance A marriage with a person of lower social status. From the French.

Marionette An articulated puppet or doll, whose jointed limbs are moved by strings. From the French: diminutive of *marie*.

Crêpe A light cotton, silk or other fabric with a fine ridge, or crinkled; A black armband originally made of this to be worn as a sign of mourning; a very thin pancake often rolled or folded round a filling. From the French.

Gasconade Boastful talk, bragging and bluster. From the French *gasconner*, to chatter.

Misère A call in solo whist where the caller undertakes to make no tricks.

Misericord A ledge projecting from the underside of the hinged seat of a choir stall in a church on which the occupant can support himself whilst standing; a relaxation of certain monastic rules for aged or infirm monks and nuns; a monastery where such relaxation can be enjoyed; also a small medieval dagger used to give the death stroke to a wounded foe. From the French: 'compassion'.

Plaque An ornamental or commemorative inscribed tablet or plate of porcelain or wood; a small flat brooch or badge as of a club. From the French *plaquier*, to plate.

Brioche A soft roll or loaf, made from a very light yeast dough, sometimes mixed with currants. From the French, *broyer*, to pound.

Bien-pensant A right-thinking person. From the French.

Limaçon A heart-shaped curve made by a point lying on a line at a fixed distance from the intersection of the line with a fixed circle, the line rotating about a point on the circumference of the circle. French: literally, 'snail'.

Ordonnance The proper disposition of the elements of a building or an artistic or literary composition; a law or decree. From the French: arrangement.

Commissionaire A uniformed doorman at a hotel or theatre. From the French.

Bouillabaisse A rich stew of fish or vegetables flavoured with spices, especially saffron. From the French, meaning 'boil down'.

Boudoir A woman's bedroom or a private sitting room. From the French, literally 'room for sulking' from *bouder*, to sulk.

Boule
1. the parliament in modern Greece; the senate of an ancient Greek city-state.
2. a pear-shaped imitation ruby or sapphire, made from synthetic corundum. From the French: 'ball'.

Chevalier A member of certain orders such as the French Legion of

Honour; the lowest title of rank in the old French nobility; a chivalrous man, gallant. From the French.

Voyeur A person who obtains sexual pleasure or excitement from the observation of sexual intercourse. From the French *voir*, to see.

Guichet A grating, hatch or small opening in a wall, especially a ticket-office window. From the French.

Croupier A person who deals and collects bets at a gaming table. From the French: 'one who rides behind another'.

Crouton A small piece of fried or toasted bread, usually served in soup. In French, a diminutive of *crout*, crust.

Poltroon An abject or contemptible coward. From the French *poultron*.

Poltergeist A spirit believed to manifest its presence by rapping and other noises and also by acts of mischief, such as throwing furniture about. From the German *poltern*, to be noisy.

Chancel The part of a church containing the altar, sanctuary and choir, usually separated from the nave and transepts by a screen.

Courier A special messenger carrying diplomatic correspondence; a person who accompanies travellers on tour, and who shows them the sights. From the French *courrier*.

Courgette A small variety of vegetable marrow, cooked and eaten as a vegetable. From the French: diminutive of *courge*, marrow.

Épée A sword similar to a foil, but with a larger guard and a heavier blade of triangular cross section. From the French: 'sword'.

Épaulette A piece of ornamental material on the shoulder of a garment, especially of a military uniform. From the French *épaule*, shoulder.

Fusil A light flintlock musket. From French *fusil*. A **fusilier** is an infantryman armed with a light musket. **Fusillade** is a rapid or continued discharge of firearms; a sudden outburst, as of criticism.

Bourgeois A member of the middle class – one who is regarded as conservative and materialistic. By Marxists he is regarded as being dominated by capitalist interests. From the French: 'burgher'.

Gulag The central and administrative department of the Soviet security service established in 1931, responsible for maintaining prisons and forced labour camps. From the Russian *corri*, labour camp.

Arrière-ban In medieval France, a summons to the king's vassals to do military service. From the French: 'a call to arms'.

Arrière-pensée An unrevealed thought or intention. From the French: 'behind thought'.

Chanson de geste One of a species of old French epic poems celebrating heroic deeds.

Chamois A sure-footed goat antelope; a soft suède leather formerly made from this animal. From the French.

Chemise An unwaisted loose-fitting garment hanging straight from the shoulders; a loose shirt-like undergarment. From the French: 'shirt'.

Chariot Any stately vehicle. From French: augmentative of *char*, a car.

Cause célèbre In French, a famous lawsuit, trial or controversy.

Chrestomathy A collection of literary passages, used in the study of language. From the Greek: 'useful to learn'.

Au fond French: fundamentally, at the bottom.

Lingua franca A language used for communication amongst people of different mother tongues.

Nom de guerre French: assumed name.

Nom de plume French: pen name.

Nacelle A streamlined enclosure on an aircraft, not part of the fuselage, to accommodate an engine, passengers and crew. From the French: 'small boat'.

Nomenclatura Name of the Soviet bureaucracy, running the Government in the erstwhile Soviet Union, akin to our Civil Service.

Apparatchik An official or bureaucrat in any organisation, but especially in the Soviet Union.

Cynosure A person or thing that attracts notice, because of brilliance or beauty. From the Greek: 'dog tail'.

Euphoria A feeling of great elation. From the Greek: 'good ability to endure'.

Yom Tov Yiddish for a festival; literally; 'a good day'.

Hacienda A ranch or large estate, in Spanish.

Hangar From the French: a large workshop or building for storing and maintaining aircraft, literally: 'a shed'.

Feuilleton The part of a European newspaper containing reviews and serialised fiction. In French: 'a sheet of paper'.

Garrison Troops who guard and maintain a base or fortified place; the place itself. From the French *garir*, to defend.

Glaive Old French word for sword.

Jaeger A marksman in certain units of the German and Austrian armies; a member of a light or mountain infantry unit in some European armies. From the German: 'a hunter'.

Cretin A mentally retarded dwarf with wide-set eyes, a broad flat nose and protruding tongue. From the French *crétin*.

Chanukah The eight-day Jewish festival.

Château In France, a country house or castle.

Crème French for cream, or any of various sweet liqueurs.

Crème brulée is a cream dessert custard covered with caramelised sugar: 'burnt cream'. **Crème caramel** is a dessert made of eggs, sugar and milk, topped with caramel. **Crème de la crème** means the very best.

Crème de menthe is a liqueur flavoured with peppermint, usually bright green in colour.

Chatelain In France, the keeper or governor of a castle. A **Chatelaine** is the mistress of a castle or fashionable household.

Cicerone A person who conducts and informs sightseers. From the Italian, meaning: 'scholar'.

Papa From the French; a child's name for 'father'.

Papillon A breed of toy spaniel with large ears. In French: 'a butterfly'.

Palisade A strong fence made of stakes driven into the ground for defence purposes. From the French: 'stake'.

Fosse A ditch or moat, especially one dug as a fortification. From the French: 'a ditch'.

Billet-doux Old fashioned love letter; from the French: 'a sweet letter'.

Écru A greyish-yellow to a light grey; the colour of unbleached linen.

Rastafari A member of a Jamaican cult that regards Rastafar, the former emperor of Ethiopia, as God; characteristic of or relating to the Rastafarians.

Blouson In French, a short jacket or top having the shape of a blouse.

Blouse A woman's shirt-like garment made of cotton or nylon. From the French.

Brume Heavy fog or mist; from the French.

Eldorado From the Spanish; a fabled city in South America, rich in treasure and sought by Spanish explorers in the sixteenth century; any place of good riches or fabulous opportunity; 'the gilded place'.

Almoner From the French *almosnier*, one who distributes alms or charity on behalf of a household or institution.

Cadenza From the Italian: a virtuoso solo passage occurring near the end of a piece of music, formerly improvised by the soloist, but now usually specially composed.

Mullah A Moslem teacher, scholar or religious leader; also used as a title of respect.

Quintet From the Italian: a group of five singers or instrumentalists, or a piece of music composed for such a group; any group of five.

Oratorio From the Italian. A dramatic but unstaged musical composition for soloists, chorus and orchestra, based on a religious theme.

Marocain In French, a fabric of ribbed crêpe; a garment made from this fabric.

Mistral A strong, cold dry wind that blows through the Rhône valley and Southern France to the Mediterranean coast, mainly in winter.

Risqué In French, bordering on indecency or impropriety – to hazard.

Croquette A savoury cake or minced meat, fish etc., fried in bread crumbs. From French *croquer*, to crunch.

Croix de Guerre A French military decoration awarded for gallantry.

Bodega Spanish: a shop selling wine and sometimes groceries, especially in a Spanish-speaking country.

Cortège A formal procession, especially a funeral one; a train of attendants, or retinue; from the French.

Fandango An old Spanish courtship dance in triple time, between a couple, who dance closely and provocatively.

Eunuch From the Greek: a man who has been castrated and acts as a guard in a harem.

Harem The part of an Oriental house reserved strictly for wives and concubines; and Moslem wives and concubines collectively. From the Arabic *harem*, forbidden place.

Begum From the Turkish: in Moslem countries, a woman of high rank, especially the widow of a prince.

Seraglio The harem of a Moslem house or palace; a sultan's palace, especially in the former Turkish empire; the wives and concubines of a Moslem.

Risotto From the Italian: a dish of rice cooked in stock and served variously with tomatoes, cheese, chicken, etc.

Risorgimento The movement for the political unification of Italy in the nineteenth century. From the Italian: 'to rise again'.

Meringue Stiffly beaten egg whites, mixed with sugar and baked often as a topping for pies, cakes etc.; a small cake or shell of this mixture, often filled with cream. From the French.

Mal de mer French for 'seasickness'.

Bonanza A source, usually sudden and unexpected, of luck or wealth. From the Spanish: literally, 'calm sea'.

Babushka A headscarf tied under the chin, worn by Russian peasant women. From Russian, meaning 'grandmother'.

Balalaika A plucked musical instrument, usually having a triangular body and three strings, used chiefly for Russian folk music.

Baklava A rich cake of Middle Eastern origin, consisting of thin layers of pastry, filled with nuts and honey. From the Turkish.

Backsheesh Money given as a tip; a present, or alms. From the Russian: 'to give'.

Halal Meat from animals killed according to Moslem law. From the Arabic: 'lawful'.

Halberd A weapon consisting of a long shaft with an axe blade and a pick topped by a spearhead used in fifteenth and sixteenth century warfare. From the French *halbebarde*.

Hakim A Moslem judge, ruler or administrator; a Moslem physician. From the Arabic *hakama*, to rule.

Frisson In French, a shudder or shiver.

Fetish Something that is believed in certain cultures to be the embodiment or habitation of a spirit or magical powers; any object or activity to which one is excessively devoted, e.g. to make a fetish of cleanliness. From the French *fetiche*.

Generalissimo Supreme commander of combined military, naval and air forces. From the Italian: superlative of 'general'.

Revanchism A foreign policy of revenge, or regaining of lost territories; desire or support of such a policy.

Cabana From the Spanish; a tent used as a dressing room by the sea.

Chaparral A dense growth of shrubs and trees. From the Spanish: 'evergreen'.

Tourniquet Any instrument or device for temporarily restricting an artery of the arm or leg to control bleeding. From the French *tourner*, to turn.

Gioconda Italian: 'smiling lady'. Renowned as da Vinci's 'Mona Lisa'.

Pizzicato To be plucked with the finger. From the Italian: 'pinched'.

Tonga A light two-shelled vehicle used in rural areas of India. From the Hindi *tanga*.

Balustrade From the French: an ornamental rail or coping with its supporting set of balusters.

Balusters Any of a set of posts supporting a rail or coping.

Boulevard A wide tree-lined road in a city, often used as a promenade. From the French.

Barricade A barrier for defence, especially one erected hastily, as during street fighting. From the French *barriquer*, to barricade.

Blasé From the French: to be indifferent to something because of familiarity or surfeit; lacking enthusiasm, bored. From the French *blaser*, to cloy.

Bandeau In French, a narrow band of ribbon, velvet, worn round the head; 'a little band'.

Banderilla A decorated barbed dart thrust into the bull's neck or shoulders. From the Spanish: 'a little banner'.

Baroque A style of architecture and decorative art that flourished throughout Europe from the late sixteenth to the early eighteenth century, characterised by extensive ornamentation.

Chiaroscuro The artistic distribution of light and dark masses in a picture. From the Italian meaning 'light and dark'.

Brasserie A bar in which drinks and food are served; a small and usually cheap restaurant. From the French *brasser*, to stir.

Brassard An identifying armband; a badge; a piece of armour for the upper arm. From the French *bras*, arm.

Chasseur In the French army, a member of a unit specially trained and equipped for swift deployment. From the French: 'huntsman'.

Gorge From the French *gorger*, to stuff oneself with food; to eat ravenously.

Tapis Tapestry or carpeting, as formerly used to cover a table in a council chamber.

Emir An independent ruler or chieftain; a military commander or governor. From the Arabic: 'commander'.

Meerschaum Used to make tobacco pipes. From the German: literally, 'sea foam'.

Nacre The technical name for mother-of-pearl; from the Italian *naccara*.

Nabob A rich, powerful, or important man; formerly a European who made a fortune in the East, especially India. From the Hindi *nawwar*.

Bint A derogatory term for a girl or woman. From the Arabic: 'daughter'.

Mahout In India and the East Indies, an elephant driver or keeper. From Sanskrit, 'of great measure', originally a title.

Machzor A Jewish prayer book, containing prescribed holiday rituals. Literally: 'a cycle'.

Madeleine A small fancy sponge cake, usually coated with jam and coconut; so named after a French pastry cook.

Madonna A description of the Virgin; in Italian: 'my lady'.

Menorah A seven-branched candlestick used in the Temple, and now an emblem of Judaism and the badge of the State of Israel.

Menu A list of dishes served at a meal or that can be ordered in a restaurant. From the French.

Vidhan Sabha Legislative assembly of any of the States of India. From the Hindi: 'law assembly'.

Ayah In East Africa and other parts of the former British Empire, a maidservant, nursemaid or governess. From the Hindi *aya*.

Madrilène A cold consommé (French) flavoured with tomato juice.

Droit de seigneur In feudal times the right of a lord to have intercourse with a vassal's bride on her wedding night. Literally: 'the right of the lord'.

Droit In French, a legal or moral right or claim, due.

Duello The art of duelling; the code of rules for duelling. From the Italian.

Duenna In Spain and Portugal, an elderly woman retained by a family to act as governess and chaperone to young girls. From the Spanish *duena*.

Faute de mieux French for 'lack of something better'.

Faux pas A social blunder or indiscretion. From the French: 'false step'.

Dryad A Greek myth: a nymph or divinity of the woods. From the Greek *druas*, a tree.

Finesse Elegant skill or style or performance; subtlety and tact in handling difficult situations. In bridge, an attempt to win a trick by assuming that a particular card is held by the appropriate opponent.

Fauteuil From the French: an armchair, the sides of which are not upholstered; a folding chair.

Milah A Hebrew word used for circumcision.

Simchath-Torah 'Rejoicing in the Law'; a Jewish festival celebrated immediately after Sukkoth to mark the completion of the annual cycle of Torah reading and its immediate recommencement.

Sayyid A Moslem claiming descent from Mohammed's grandson Husain; a Moslem honorary title.

Milieu Surroundings, location or setting. In French: 'a place'.

Fata Morgana From the Italian: a mirage in the Straits of Messina, attributed to sorcery.

Parti pris A preconceived opinion. From the French: 'side taken'.

Shinto Indigenous religion of Japan, polytheistic in character and incorporating the worship of a number of ethnic divinities, from the chief of which the emperor is believed to be descended. From the Chinese: 'god's way'.

Abbé A French abbot; a title used in addressing any other French cleric.

Geisha A professional female companion for men in Japan, trained in music, dancing, and the art of conversation. From the Japanese: 'art person'.

Gegenschein A faint glow in the sky, visible at a position opposite to that of the sun. From the German: 'opposite light'.

Gefilte fish In Jewish cookery, a dish consisting of fish and matza meal rolled into balls and poached. From the Yiddish: filled fish.

Gehenna A place where the wicked are punished after death; a place or state of torment. From the Hebrew: 'valley of hell'.

Gelt In Yiddish: money or cash.

Gemara In Judaism, the main body of the Talmud consisting of a record of ancient rabbinical debates about the interpretation of the Mishna, and constituting the primary source of Jewish religious law. From the Aramaic: 'completion'.

Seljuk A member of any of the pre-Ottoman Turkish dynasties, ruling over large parts of Asia, in the eleventh to thirteenth centuries. From the Turkish.

Selva A dense equatorial forest. From Spanish and Portuguese.

Mihrab Niche in a mosque showing the direction of Mecca. From the Arabic.

Chapter 32

Esperanto is the world auxiliary language and was invented by a Polish Jew, an oculist, Dr Lazarus Ludwig Zamenhof. He was born in 1859 in Bialystok which at that time was part of the Russian Empire. The town was inhabited by Poles, Jews, Germans and Russians. Zamenhof pondered deeply over the hostility which the various groups displayed towards each other, and came to the conclusion that this hostility was due to the fact that they did not understand each other, because they spoke different languages.

On a wider scale nations did not understand each other, and this was the reason they waged war against each other.

In Zamenhof's time, travelling was far more restricted than it is nowadays, though ladies and gentlemen had been making what was known as the Grand Tour to Italy and especially Rome, for some centuries. Macaulay has described in vivid prose his delight in making this tour. 'All roads lead to Rome', so to speak, and of course, the travellers had had a classical education and Latin was their language, as of course it has been for many centuries for the Catholic Church. In the Anglican Church this also has been the case; Latin is the international language.

It is interesting to note that there has been a disagreement in the Church between Cardinal Lefèbre and the Papacy over the use or non-use of Latin in some of the prayers. The issue was decided not in the Cardinal's favour.

Zamenhof decided to make Esperanto as simple as possible to European nations. This meant that the language would be harder for Asians and Africans, but he could not make it easier for them without making it harder for Europeans. He decided that Europe must come first; if he could not sell the product there, to use a commercial metaphor, his language would fail.

The language was offered to the world in 1887. It did not, however, have a world-wide enthusiastic reception, as one might have thought it should. One reason for this was the growing pressure of American English. One might say that the influence of American power economically and politically upon the rest of the world has brought in its train a sort of linguistic imperialism. This power is asserting that American English is the world language and should be accepted as such. The smaller nations in the world, such as Holland, Belgium, Luxembourg and Scandinavian countries have recognised that their languages have no great standing in the world, and have accepted this argument.

We find on examining the languages of small nations a most extraordinary case in the language of the Basque Provinces. The language of the Basques has no known relationship with any other autonomous region of northern Spain comprising the provinces of Alava, Guipozcoa and Viscaya. The Basques had retained virtual autonomy from the ninth to the nineteenth centuries. They are now in conflict with the Spanish Government which wishes to deprive them of this autonomy, and the Basques, with their language Euskarl are, in true Spanish style, waging guerila warfare; the conflict has been raging for some years now and there is no end in sight.

Notwithstanding this there have been riots and strife between two groups in Belgium, one of which favours French and the other Flemish, a language closely allied to Dutch.

The attitude of the supporters of American English is contradictory; whilst they support it, they still maintain the need to teach other languages, such as French, German and Spanish.

It is interesting to note that the Japanese in their capacity of being an economic superpower are not making any effort to spread the usage of their language; they realise that the difficulties encountered by prospective learners are insuperable; only a very small number of gifted linguists could succeed. It is possible that the Japanese might try to emulate the example of Turkey, which has abandoned its Arabic alphabet in favour of the Latin one. There is even talk that the Congress of Independent States (CIS) is considering switching its Cyrillic alphabet in favour of Latin. It is very hard to imagine that the CIS would ever agree to do this; it would be a blow to their pride, but one cannot tell if the severity of the economic crisis, which is worsening all the time, will affect their future action.

It is interesting to note that tiny Switzerland is divided into four regions, each of which speaks a different language: French, German, Italian and Romansch. It was a leading centre of the Reformation. Since its inception it has adopted a policy of strict neutrality in all wars regardless of the nationality of the combatants. In the fifteenth century the Swiss were notorious for being mercenaries. They took part in a battle against the Duke of Burgundy at Nancy in 1477. The Duke was killed in this battle and the King of France, Louis XI (1461–1483) could heave a deep sigh of relief at being free from attack by a powerful adversary. In the fifteenth and sixteenth centuries, Zwingli (1484–1531) and John Calvin, leader of the Protestant Reformation in France and Switzerland, established the first Presbyterian Government in Geneva. Their system em-braced the doctrine of predestination, the irresistibility of grace and justification by faith. The reformation had begun as an attempt to reform the Roman Catholic Church.

Martin Luther (1483–1546) had been a professor of biblical theology at Wittenberg University. In 1517 he nailed 95 theses to the church door at Wittenberg. He attacked the Papacy for sending Tetzel to Germany to sell indulgences. This meant that by paying money to the Papacy, people would be able to obtain the release of their deceased relatives from Purgatory. For his attack, Luther was excommunicated and outlawed by the Diet of Worms (1521). He had refused to recant.

But he had powerful friends, among them Frederick of Saxony. When the peasants' war broke out in 1525, Luther strongly opposed them. Peasants were peasants and, irrespective of their religious beliefs, must not rebel against their masters. Luther was a rabid antisemite and the instigator of pogrom-like measures against Jews; on one occasion he hurled an inkpot into the air, saying that he was fighting the devils. It is impossible to understand the meaning of this remark. His most important work was the translation of the Bible into German.

Chapter 33

We are living today in an era of continual international conferences, where heads of governments and their foreign ministers, together with military, scientific, economic and political advisers, meet regularly to discuss not only their own problems, from a national point of view, but from a point of view acceptable to all.

With the ending of the Cold War, which had begun in 1945, there are no longer any power blocs hostile to each other. The United States is accepted as the leading nation in the world, and in the United Nations. The latter has taken over from the old League of Nations which proved, at a time of crises, to be ineffective. This was the case in 1935, when Italy invaded Ethiopia and the League of Nations endeavoured to apply sanctions against the supply of oil to Italy.

Nowadays, the position is vastly different; the nations have come to the conclusion that an international authority is essential and must be given military support whenever necessary. The present crisis with Iraq and its dictator Saddam Hussein shows the importance of military power to enforce its decisions and rulings. The need for this has been strongly reinforced by the present situation in Yugoslavia, where civil war, or 'ethnic cleansing', has been raging for over a year. The United Nations is very occupied with watching the unfolding of events there and elsewhere.

One would have thought that the members of the UN would appreciate the desirability of a common language in which to conduct their affairs. There are at present a number of Western languages involved. The non-European members have to learn at least one European language, at present English.

How much more convenient and efficient the use of Esperanto would be. This would not only be far more economical, but would have the important psychological effect of relieving the feeling of inferiority of the smaller nations, that their own language is unimportant. It would be the end of what we have previously described as linguistic imperialism. What a wonderful thing it would be for all nationalities, perhaps several hundred, to meet and discuss world affairs in a position of complete linguistic equality.

Chapter 34

The language

Alphabet

a   as in English
b   as in English
c   as ts in cats
ĉ   as ch in church
d
e   as in met
f
g   as in get
ĝ   as in jet
i   as in miss
j   as y in yacht
ĵ   as su in pleasure
k   as in kipper
l   as in let
m   as in mail
n   as in nib
o   as in hold
p   as in pod
r   as in rail
s   as in soft
ŝ   as sh in ship
u   as u in rude
v   as v in veal
z   as in zebra

Infinitive verbs all end in -*i*, for example:
    skribi   to write
    trinki   to drink
    labori   to work

The present tense ends in -*as* for all persons:
    skribas, trinkas, laboras

The past ends in -*is*:
    skribis, trinkis, laboris

The future ends in -*os*:
    skribos, trinkos, laboros

The conditional ends in -*us*:
    skribus, trinkus, laborus

The imperative ends in -*u*:
    skribu, trinku, laboru

la = the

Adjectives end in -*a* in the singular and -*aj* (pronounced 'aye') in the plural.
Nouns end in -*o* in the singular, and -*oj* (pronounced 'oye') in the plural.

mi	= I	ci	= thou	li	= he	ŝi	= she
ni	= we	vi	= you	ili	= they		
oni	= one (not a numeral, but as in English: 'one does'.)						

la bonay knabo   =   the good boy
la bonaj knaboj   =   the good boys

Esperanto uses only one case: the accusative.
Mi vidas   la knubon = I see the boy
This eliminates any possibility of error.

Every verb has *one* meaning only. This is Esperanto's great achievement. It removes the bane of language. Every national language has developed like an untended garden where the weeds are allowed to grow so that in time, they stifle the natural products of the garden. Order must be maintained if the garden is to flourish; Esperanto prevents the formation of weeds; in this respect, it acts as a super gardener.

We have examined a number of cases previously where verbs have double and contradictory meanings. This is impossible in Esperanto.

Esperanto is very easy to learn. If children in school were to start learning Esperanto from the age of eight or nine, by the time they were fifteen or so the overwhelming majority would have a fluent command of it. Their knowledge of French, German or Spanish at this age would by comparison by only slight. Even at A level, their command of any of these languages would still be only minimal; it is doubtful whether they could communicate effectively on relatively simple matters with the native people.

It is difficult to understand why governments cannot see the enormous practical advantages which the use of Esperanto would bring.

We must hope that Esperanto, which means 'one who hopes', will see this hope soon realised.